Introduction

Surprise was always one of the key elements of success during offensive air operations, be it counter-air, bombing/attack or reconnaissance missions. Accordingly, it was vital for those on the receiving end to learn of the enemy's approach in advance. Originally the side being attacked had to rely on human observers and telephone or radio communication. The development of radar technology made possible the advent of radar picket ships; the next obvious step was to develop a technology initially known as airborne early warning (AEW). A key function of such flying radar pickets – control of 'friendly' fighters or strike aircraft – soon led the designation to be amended to airborne early warning and control (AEW&C) or airborne warning and control system (AWACS).

Development of AEW aircraft began in earnest after the Second World War. Initially the USA and Great Britain were the main developers and users of this technology. Shipboard AEW aircraft intended for protecting naval task forces (especially aircraft carriers, which are vulnerable and lucrative targets) were of necessity compact because of space constraints during on-deck storage or below-deck stowage. The shore-based ones, on the other hand, were unencumbered by such limitations and could be based on transport aircraft or airliners, offering greater fuel capacity (which meant longer endurance) and room for a relief crew.

Thus, in 1949 Lockheed Aircraft brought out a radar picket version of the L-749 Constellation piston-engined airliner designated PO-1W (later WV-1); a more advanced version based on the L-1049 Constellation followed in 1953 as the WV-2 Warning Star, becoming the EC-121K in 1962. A successor to the Warning Star was developed, using the Boeing 707-320B four-turbofan airliner as the basis. Originally known as the EC-137D and subsequently redesignated E-3A Sentry, this aircraft first flew in 1972 and entered service in 1977. Unlike the predecessor, which had conventional fixed radomes, it had the surveillance radar antennas mounted in a distinctive lentil-shaped revolving housing – a so-called rotodome – carried above the fuselage on twin pylons. A succession of versions with ever more capable avionics (and, later, new CFM56-2A2 engines) was brought out; the E-3 is arguably the best-known AWACS aircraft which, apart from the US Air Force, has seen service with the NATO's AEW Force in Europe, the air arms of the UK, France and Saudi Arabia. As a successor to the Sentry, in 1991 Boeing developed the E-767 based on the Boeing 767-200ER twin-turbofan airliner; the type entered limited production in 1992.

Meanwhile, in the Soviet Union the airborne early warning issue was taken equally seriously; the Soviet political and military leaders were reasonably well informed on military technology development in the West – and on the strengths and flaws of their own

A Tu-126 AWACS of the 67th Independent AEW Squadron in flight.

A Tu-126 is shadowed over the Mediterranean Sea by Douglas A-4E Skyhawk BuNo 152012 (AU-652) of attack squadron VA-45/Det.1 'Blackbirds' from the aircraft carrier USS *Intrepid* in 1973.

national air defence system, too. As the West developed new offensive weapon systems capable of striking across the North Pole, the northern and Far Eastern regions of the Soviet Union were no longer safe. Building and operating airbases and air defence (AD) radar systems in those parts was difficult, if not impossible, due to the harsh climatic conditions and logistics problems. To close that hole in the Soviet air defence network, the Air Defence Force (PVO – **Pro**tivovoz-**doosh**naya obo**ron**a) needed AEW&C assets comparable to those developed in the West.

On 4th July 1958 the Soviet Council of Ministers (= government) issued a directive tasking OKB-156 (**opy**tno-kon**strook**torskoye byu**ro** – experimental design bureau) headed by General Designer Andrey N. Tupolev with creating an AWACS aircraft. The aircraft was to be designed around the newly-developed *Liana* (Creeper) radar/communications suite created by the Moscow Research Institute of Instrument Engineering (NII-17, or MNIIP – *Mos***kov**skiy na**ooch**no-is**sled**ovatel'skiy insti**toot** pri**bor**ostro**yen**iya) under General Designer Vladimir P. Ivanov. The Liana radar had phenomenal performance by the day's standards; detection range in the upper hemisphere was to be 100 km (62 miles) for a fighter-size target, 200 km (124 miles) for a tactical bomber and 300 km (186 miles) for a strategic bomber. Detection range below the horizon, however, was limited to only 20 km (12.4 miles).

The Tupolev Tu-114 *Ros***si**ya (Russia) four-turboprop long-haul airliner (NATO reporting name *Cleat*) was selected as the mission platform for the Soviet AWACS. Designated Tu-126 or *iz***del**iye L ('product L' – a reference to the Liana suite), the aircraft had

the radar array in a rotodome mounted on a thick single pylon about halfway between the wings and the vertical tail; it was the world's first aircraft to feature a rotodome. Radiation shielding was applied to protect the crew from the powerful high-frequency radiation generated by the mission equipment. The Tu-126 had a flight crew of six and a mission crew of six; a relief crew was also carried. Additionally, the aircraft was equipped with a probe-and-drogue in-flight refuelling (IFR) system allowing it to remain airborne for up to 11 hours.

The prototype was completed in late 1961, making its first flight on 23rd February 1962. Due to the very special mission fulfilled by the aircraft only eight production Tu-126s were built in 1965-67. On 30th April 1965 the type was formally included the into the PVO inventory, serving with the 67th Independent AEW Squadron based at Siauliai (pronounced '**Sha**ooliay'), Latvia. The NATO's Air Standards Co-ordinating Committee (ASCC) allocated the reporting name *Moss* (in the 'miscellaneous aircraft' category) to the Tu-126; the Liana radar also had a codename, *Flat Jack*.

Unfortunately the Tu-126 remained viable as an early warning and control system only until the end of the 1960s. By then NATO strike aircraft had gained the ability to penetrate Soviet airspace at low and ultra-low altitudes; detecting such low-flying intruders at acceptable range was beyond the Tu-126's capabilities, as the Liana radar had very limited 'look-down' capability against low-flying targets. As a result, development of a new AWACS was initiated, this effort eventually resulting in the subject of this book – the Il'yushin/Beriyev A-50.

Acknowledgements
The book is illustrated with photos by: Yefim Gordon, Sergey Krivchikov, Konstantin Tyurpeko, Aleksandr Beltyukov, Dmitriy Pichugin, Sergey Sergeyev, Sergey Skrynnikov, Viktor Drushlyakov, Sergey Balakleyev, Mikhail Gribovskiy, the Royal Swedish Air Force, as well as from the archives of TANTK Beriyev and the Tupolev PLC, the personal archive of Yefim Gordon, as well as from the following web sites: www.fyjs.cn, www.concentric.net, www.sinodefence.com, www.cjdby.net, www.pic.chinamil.com.cn, www.flankers-site.co.uk, www.airlinercafe.com, www.amercom-hobby.com, www.karopka.ru, www.scalemates.com, www.hsfeatures.com, www.scalemodels.ru, www.airfixtributeforum.myfastforum.org, www.brazmodels.com, www.findmodelkit.com, www.flyingmule.com, www.gregers.fr.yuku.com, www.diecastaircraftforum.com, www.modelversium.de, www.ebay.com and www.aoqi2014.en.made-in-china.com. Line drawings by Andrey Yurgenson. Colour drawings by Aleksandr Gavrilov and Andrey Yurgenson.

Enter the Bumblebee:
A-50 – the 'Domestic' Versions

The Soviet military recognised the need to develop a successor to the Tu-126 when the latter had barely entered production. A new-generation AWACS had to be ready for service by the time the Tu-126 had gathered moss – as it would have by the early 1980s. Besides, the Boeing E-3A Sentry was superior to the *Moss* on all counts. Therefore, in 1969 the Soviet Council of Ministers sanctioned the development of a successor to the Liana mission avionics suite with enhanced 'look-down' capability that would be capable of detecting and tracking low-flying targets, including terrain-following cruise missiles.

Actually, work on the new suite designated Shmel' (Bumblebee) had begun at MNIIP as early as 1966; again, Vladimir P. Ivanov headed the development effort. The suite was built around a coherent pulse-Doppler 360° surveillance radar of the same name. The components of the suite were manufactured by plants scattered far and wide across the nation; integration was performed by the Tashkent Electronics Plant.

The Shmel' radar was able to track up to 50 targets at a time over land and water, with a maximum range of 230 km (142 miles); large targets like surface ships could be detected and tracked at up to 400 km (248 miles). The radar set used high-power klystrons; the signals were processed by a quite of four digital computers. The radar operated in quasi-continuous mode when tracking aerial targets and in pulse mode when tracking maritime targets; in the former case three similar pulse rate frequencies (PRFs) were used to enhance ranging accuracy. Ground clutter was suppressed by selecting the most appropriate frequencies. Ivanov claimed the Shmel' had shorter detection range but better resistance to ground clutter than the Westinghouse

AN/APY-1 fitted to the Boeing E-3A. The suite also included an active identification friend-or-foe (IFF) system, a data processing and presentation system, data storage equipment and secure digital communications/data link equipment for communicating with ground and shipboard command, control, communications and intelligence (C^3I) centres and friendly fighters.

Naturally, the issue of a suitable platform for the Shmel' suite arose. The Tupolev OKB offered a 'clean sheet of paper' design – the four-turbofan '156' (Tu-156) aircraft strongly resembling the E-3A; however, this was rejected by the Air Force, which insisted that an aircraft already in production should be used.

In the meantime, however, other Soviet aircraft design bureaux, including OKB-240 headed by Sergey V. Il'yushin (now known as the Il'yushin Aviation Complex), were also working on AWACS platforms. On 7th August 1969 the CofM Presidium's Commission on Defence Industry Matters (VPK – *Voyenno-promyshlennaya komissiya*) issued a ruling requiring the Il'yushin OKB to undertake preliminary development of an AWACS aircraft tentatively designated **Il-70**. This aircraft, the second project thus designated (the Il-70 designation had been used in 1961-63 for a 24-seat twin-turbojet regional airliner), was a derivative of the Il-76 *Candid* four-turbofan heavy transport. The latter was as-yet unflown, much less in production; however, the project was then at a very advanced stage (the design was frozen in December that year), and as the Soviet Air Force needed the Il-76 anyway the type was sure to enter mass production, so the military decided to stretch a point.

Presently the Il-76 prototype made its first flight on 25th March 1971, and after

A desktop model of the proposed Tu-156 AWACS looking remarkably like the Boeing E-3.

The antenna array of the Shmel' surveillance radar during bench tests.

One of the two dielectric sections of the RA-10 rotodome. As the photo shows, the rotodome was deep enough to stand in. Note that the huge dielectric structure is composed of many small panels.

naoochno-tekhnicheskiy **kompleks** – the Taganrog Aviation Scientific & Technical Complex named after Gheorgiy M. Beriyev), which was to act as systems integrator. Hence the new AWACS received the 'non-Il'yushin' designation **A-50** and the in-house product code *izdeliye* A; compare this to the Beriyev A-40 Albatross (NATO *Mermaid*) anti-submarine warfare amphibian. Had Il'yushin alone been responsible for the job, the designation would have been something like Il-76RLD (**rah**diolokatsi**onnyy** do**zor** – radar picket) – or Il-70. Hence Western aviation experts tend to attribute the A-50 solely to the Beriyev OKB – although, in fairness, the Il'yushin OKB should be listed as a 'co-author'. Beriyev OKB Chief Designer Aleksey K. Konstantinov exercised overall control of the integration/debugging effort, his deputy Sergey A. Atayants being appointed the A-50's project chief.

The main structural change was the conventionally located RA-10 rotodome housing a slotted antenna array measuring 10 x 1.7 m (32 ft 9⁴⁵⁄₆₄ in x 5 ft 6⁵⁹⁄₆₄ in). Mounted on twin tapered pylons immediately aft of the wings, it had a diameter of 10.8 m (35 ft 5³⁄₁₆ in) and was some 2 m (6 ft 6¾ in) deep; there were two large dielectric portions of equal size, only the constant-chord narrow centre portion being made of metal. (In contrast, the Tu-126's rotodome of 11 m (36 ft 1 in) diameter and 2 m (6 ft 6¾ in) deep was mostly a metal structure with one dielectric portion.) The rotodome was located more than one diameter ahead of and well below the horizontal tail, which was important in view of the Il-76's T-tail. The lift generated by the rotodome increased the downwash on the stabilisers, reducing their efficiency, but the rotodome itself contributed a stabilising influence. Also, wake turbulence from the rotodome reduced the efficiency of the vertical tail but the rotodome pylons made up for this – albeit at the expense of reduced lateral stability because of the additional sideforce above the centre of gravity.

The need to accommodate the mission equipment led to other airframe changes. The extensive glazing of the navigator's station characteristic of the Il-76 was replaced by a large dielectric fairing, leaving the A-50 with only a single small window on each side. The weather radar's radome was slightly smaller and had a reshaped joint line, with two small dielectric panels on either side aft of it.

The standard Il-76 has two entry doors that can be used for paradropping personnel; on the A-50, however, the port side door was deleted as unnecessary. So was the tail gunner's station of the *Candid-B* which gave way to an avionics bay, with two aft-facing dielectric fairings where the UKU-9K-502 cannon barbette and the glazing used to be; a large cooling air intake for the equipment in the rear bay was added at the base of the fin. The three-segment cargo doors were faired over; the cargo ramp remained but was non-functional.

two years of extensive testing the type entered production at aircraft factory No.84 in Tashkent. With its high speed, payload and range the Il-76 looked set to be an excellent AWACS platform. True, an airliner-type platform like the E-3 – or the stillborn Tu-156 – would have higher flight performance. However, the Il-76 offered ample space for the mission avionics and mission crew (no small thing, since Soviet avionics were typically bulkier than their Western counterparts); also, its high-flotation landing gear allowed it to operate from semi-prepared runways, which might be a requirement in times of war. Furthermore, once the Il-76 *Candid-B* military transport had entered service on a mass scale and the inevitable teething troubles had been overcome, there would be fewer operational problems with its special-mission derivative. Thus, in 1973 the Communist Party Central Committee and the Council of Ministers issued a joint directive officially specifying the Il-76 as the basis for the new AWACS.

In addition to MNIIP (later known as NPO Vega-M; NPO = *naoochno-proizvodstvennoye obyedineniye* – Scientific & Production Corporation), the Il'yushin OKB teamed up with the Beriyev OKB based in Taganrog, southern Russia (now known as TANTK Beriyev, *Taganrogskiy aviatsionnyy*

The lateral fairings enclosing the main landing gear fulcrums and actuators were modified considerably to house some of the equipment. The front ends of these fairings were fatter and blunter than those of the Il-76, each incorporated two circular air intakes of unequal size, with outlet gills further aft. This required the TA-6 auxiliary power unit (APU) to be relocated from the front portion of the port fairing to its rear end, the lateral intake door and exhaust giving place to a dorsal 'elephant's ear' intake and a downward-angled exhaust.

The A-50 bristled with various antennas. Four ECM antennas in large teardrop fairings were located on the forward and aft fuselage sides to give 360° coverage; a large dorsal dielectric fairing ahead of the wing leading edge housed satellite communications (SATCOM) antennas. Numerous blade aerials were located on the forward fuselage and ahead of the cargo ramp, and two large strake aerials were fitted aft of the nose gear. Downward-firing chaff/flare dispensers were incorporated into the rear fuselage for self-protection.

Like its predecessor (the Tu-126), the A-50 was provided with a telescopic IFR probe located ahead of the flight deck glazing, with an external fuel conduit running along the starboard side above the entry door to the wings. For night refuelling the probe was illuminated by retractable lights, a standard feature on Soviet heavy aircraft using the probe-and-drogue system.

The fully pressurised cargo hold was converted into a mission crew cabin and an avionics bay. The A-50 had a flight crew of five (two pilots, a flight engineer, a navigator and a radio operator) and a mission crew of ten – the mission crew chief, the senior radar operator (RO) responsible for tracking targets, two regular ROs, the senior radar intercept officer (RIO) responsible for guiding 'friendly' interceptors, two regular RIOs and three mission equipment engineers. The RIO and RO workstations featured colour cathode-ray tube (CRT) displays. To protect the crew from the electromagnetic pulses generated by the radar, most of the windows (except the flight deck windscreens) had gold plating.

When designing the A-50 the Il'yushin and Beriyev OKBs had to deal with numerous problems that were quite new to them, or at least had been encountered on a much smaller scale. These were most associated with the mission avionics and the various ancillary systems. With so many powerful transmitters and sensitive receivers crammed into a relatively small space, the electromagnetic compatibility (EMC) problem loomed large and had to be taken care of by building a special ground test rig. The Shmel' suite passed extensive testing on the Tu-126LL avionics testbed (*letayushchaya laboratoriya* – lit. 'flying laboratory', a Russian term used indiscriminately for any kind of testbed or research/survey aircraft) converted from the Tu-126 prototype in 1977

(also known as LL 'A' – that is, testbed for *izdeliye* A). Air and liquid cooling systems, the likes of which had not been seen in the USSR before, were created, as was a special electric system supplying power with highly stable parameters for the mission equipment. Additionally, a large amount of wind tunnel work was done to make sure that the rotodome did not impair the aircraft's stability and handling to an unacceptable degree.

Meanwhile, a production Il-76 *sans suffixe* (*Candid-B*) registered CCCP-76641 (c/n 073409243, f/n 0701) and operated by the Beriyev OKB was selected for conversion as

Above: A complete RA-10 rotodome undergoing static tests.

Below: One of the two dielectric sections of the rotodome on a ground handling dolly.

'10 Red', the first prototype A-50, at Taganrog-Yoozhnyy. This three-quarters rear view shows the dielectric fairings supplanting the gunner's station, the cooling air intake at the base of the fin and the aft-positioned APU with an 'elephant's ear' air intake.

the first prototype A-50. (**Note:** Il-76 and A-50 construction numbers are deciphered as follows. The first two or three digits denote the year of manufacture: here, 07 = 1977. The next two digits are always 34, a code for factory No.84. The remaining five digits do not signify *anything at all* so that the c/n would not reveal how many aircraft have been built; the first two and the final three of these 'famous last five' accrue independently. Additionally, the aircraft have *fuselage numbers* (or line numbers) allowing the manufacturer to keep track of production; in this case, 0701 = Batch 07, 01st aircraft of ten in the batch.)

Wearing a distinctive grey/white colour scheme and Soviet Air Force insignia but no

tactical code, the first prototype A-50 was completed in 1978 and made its maiden flight at Taganrog-Yoozhnyy (= Taganrog-South) on 19th December, captained by test pilot Vladimir P. Dem'yanovskiy; M. D. Koreshkov was the engineer in charge of the tests. At the initial flight test phase the aircraft had neither mission avionics nor the IFR probe. When the Shmel' suite was presently installed, for a while the first prototype effectively became a ground test rig used for debugging the mission avionics which were extremely troublesome at first and suffered from EMC problems.

Two more A-50 prototypes were converted from *Candid-Bs* at Taganrog by Octo-

The first prototype in a test flight over the Black Sea. Note the white-tipped nose unique to this aircraft. All dielectric fairings except the rotodome are painted white.

Above and below: The second prototype, '15 Red', at Taganrog-Yoozhnyy, showing the different nose treatment with additional small square dielectric inserts ahead of the navigator's station window. The dielectric parts are still mostly white. The distinctively shaped fat front ends of the main gear fairings with twin cooling air intakes are clearly visible; in contrast, the rear ends are still standard IL-76 style at this stage.

Above: An early artist's impression of the A-50 from a Western aeronautical magazine, showing the rotodome mounted on a Tu-126 style single pylon and the gunner's station.

that the fuselage was stretched ahead of the wings (which it wasn't). An early drawing even showed the rotodome mounted on a single short pylon *à la* Tu-126.

The joint state acceptance trials (i.e., certification trials performed jointly by the manufacturer and the military) took place in 1980-85 at Vladimirovka airbase in Akhtoobinsk near Saratov, southern Russia – the main facility of the Soviet Air Force State Research Institute named after Valeriy P. Chkalov (GK NII VVS – *Gosudarstvennyy Krasnoznamyonnyy naoochno-issledovatel'skiy instituot Voyenno-vozdooshnykh seel*). The prototypes were also seen at Chkalovskaya AB near Moscow, which hosts another GK NII VVS branch. The State commission holding the trials was chaired by none other than Soviet Air Force C-in-C Air Chief Marshal Pavel S. Kutakhov, a fact that testified to the degree of importance attached to the A-50. Minister of Aircraft Industry Ivan S. Silayev and Minister of Electronics Industry Pyotr S. Pleshakov also kept a tab on the A-50's progress.

ber 1983; these were coded '15 Red' (c/n 073410311, f/n 0808) and '20 Red' (c/n 0013430875, f/n 2209A). The first prototype, which was coded '10 Red' in due course, was used for performance/handling tests and testing the ancillary systems; the second machine served for verifying the Shmel' suite and the *Poonkteer* (Dotted line) navigation suite, while the third one was used for ECM equipment trials.

Western intelligence got wind of the A-50's development in 1983 and the aircraft was allocated the unusually laudatory reporting name *Mainstay*. At first, however, the West had a rather vague idea of what the aircraft looked like; artist's impressions showed a conventional glazed nose and tail gunner's station, and there have been claims

Longitudinal stability problems cropped up at an early stage; to remedy this, two large horizontal strakes of quasi-triangular planform were added to the aft portions of the main gear fairings on production *Mainstays*. Also, it turned out that in-flight refuelling was all but impossible because the rotodome would hit wake turbulence from the tanker, causing severe buffeting. On internal fuel the A-50 had an endurance of four hours at

Right: '20 Red', the third and final prototype. Note the slightly different nose markings with a white stripe below the anti-glare panel.

Opposite page: An early-production A-50 *sans suffixe* shows the characteristic horizontal strakes added to the rear ends of the main gear fairings. On production aircraft the colour division line is positioned lower and the dielectric panels (except the small ones on the nose) are painted grey.

This page:
A-50 '40 Red' intercepted by a Royal Swedish Air Force fighter over international waters. The IFR probe appears to have been removed from this aircraft, leaving only a stub.

'41 Red', an operational A-50 *sans suffixe*, making a surprise visit to Kubinka AB near Moscow. The outer engines' thrust reversers are deployed, the flaps are fully extended and tailplane trim is very much in evidence.

Two more views of the same aircraft parked near the hardware demonstration facility hangar at Kubinka. Note the extreme wear and tear on the rotodome, the green primer showing through the grey pain on the upper side.

Opposite page:
A KrAZ-255B prime mover pushes back A-50 '47 Red' onto its hardstand at the Russian Air Force's 929th State Flight Test Centre (Vladimirovka AB, Akhtoobinsk), in 1994. A TZ-22 articulated fuel bowser stands by to refuel the aircraft for the next mission.

A production A-50 *sans suffixe* takes off at Akhtoobinsk.

Above and below:
A rather weathered
uncoded A-50,
probably an early-
production machine,
stored on the TANTK
Beriyev apron at
Taganrog-Yoozhnyy.

1,000 km (620 miles) from base; maximum take-off weight was 190,000 kg (418,875 lb).

The trials results were generally positive, and in December 1984 the A-50 was ordered into production at plant No.84, which by then had been renamed Tashkent Aircraft Production Corporation named after Valeriy P. Chkalov (TAPO – *Tashkentskoye aviatsionnoye proizvodstvennoye obyedineniye*). The latter manufactured 'green' A-50 airframes bearing the in-house designation **Il-76A**, which were then flown to Taganrog-Yoozhnyy for outfitting at plant No.86, aka TMZD (*Taganrogskiy mashinostroitel'nyy zavod imeni Dimitrova* – Taganrog Machinery Plant named after Gheorgi Dimitrov).

Deliveries to the PVO commenced in 1985; the 67th Independent AEW Squadron progressively re-equipped with A-50s, allowing the Tu-126 to be withdrawn, and the operational evaluation stage lasted until 1988. During this time the flights were confined to Soviet territory. The first sighting over international waters did not take place until 4th December 1987 when a Royal Norwegian Air Force (333 Sqn) Lockheed P-3B Orion from Bodø AB encountered an uncoded A-50 over the Barents Sea.

Production proceeded at a rate of one to five aircraft per year until 1989. The three prototypes were followed by 19 production A-50 *sans suffixe* in batches 27, 32, 35, 37-

41, 44, 45, 50, 52, 55, 57, 58, 60 and 62-64; for some obscure reason all of them were the fifth aircraft in their respective batches. They wore the tactical codes '30 Red' through '43 Red' and '46 Red' through '49 Red' allocated in random order. In 1989 the A-50 was officially included into the PVO inventory. Later, when the existence of new versions was revealed, the reporting name of the original A-50 *sans suffixe* was amended to *Mainstay-A*.

Il'yushin, Beriyev and NPO Vega-M kept working on refining the *Mainstay* – primarily improving reliability and reducing avionics weight (Soviet avionics weighed about 50% more than their Western counterparts,

hence the old joke about Soviet microchips being the largest microchips in the world). Work on an upgraded mission avionics suite for the A-50 began when the aircraft had just begun its evaluation stage.

On 9th January 1984 the Communist Party Central Committee and the Council of Ministers issued a joint directive ordering the Beriyev OKB to develop the **A-50M** AWACS (*moderni**zee**rovannyy* – updated). Known in-house as *izdeliye* 2A, the A-50M was to have a Shmel'-2 mission avionics suite, a much more capable navigation suite and enhanced ECM capability. Besides detecting and tracking a greater number of targets at longer range, the Shmel'-2 mission avionics suite

Above and below:
Pictured at Akhtoobinsk, the A-50M prototype, '44 Red', shows off the characteristic strap-on IRCM flare dispensers and the additional ECM blister fairings aft of them. Note the soot deposits on the rear fuselage caused by the APU running in flight.

was to enable co-operative intercepts by a larger number of 'friendly' fighters.

Another important change concerned the powerplant. Instead of the 12,000-kgp (26,455-lbst) D-30KP turbofans used hitherto the A-50M was to feature D-90 turbofans then under development at the Solov'yov OKB for the Tu-204 medium-haul airliner (the engine was renamed PS-90 in 1987). The D-90 had a higher bypass ratio and a cascade-type thrust reverser with a translating cowl instead of a clamshell thrust reverser. Initially delivering 12,500 kgp (27,560 lbst), it was uprated to 15,000 kgp (33,070 lbst) and then to 16,000 kgp (35,270 lbst) in due course, which held promise of a major performance boost.

The work proceeded rapidly; the A-50M project was completed before the end of 1984 and a full-size mock-up was built that year. Deputy Chief Designer Sergey A. Atayants supervised the project development, with I. V. Kalinin as the project chief. The components of the Shmel'-2 suite were put through their paces on the suitably modified Tu-126LL testbed, which was now known as the LL '2A'. Meanwhile, TAPO started construction of the A-50M prototype which was to enter flight test in 1989.

However, the economic crisis that followed in the wake of Mikhail S. Gorbachov's new *perestroika* policy ruined these plans.

Development problems with the PS-90 engine were probably another contributing factor – the envisaged powerplant was not available on time, although the Il'yushin Il-96-300 long-haul airliner and the Tupolev Tu-204 medium-haul airliner powered by PS-90s had entered flight test in September 1988 and January 1989 respectively. On 22nd October 1990 the Council of Ministers issued a directive suspending all further work on the A-50M due to lack of funds.

Therefore, the A-50M as actually built was a more modest upgrade, retaining the standard D-30KP engines. Its external recognition features distinguishing it from the A-50 *sans suffixe* are the lack of the navigator's station window to port (only the starboard window remains), two additional dielectric blisters on the rear fuselage sides near the cargo ramp, the areas of matt off-white paint aft of these extra blisters and ahead of the forward ECM blisters, and the strap-on 96-round chaff/flare dispensers on the rear fuselage sides augmenting the built-in dispensers for extra protection against air-to-air and surface-to-air missiles. These dispensers are of a different type from the APP-50 strap-on pods of identical capacity fitted to late-production Il-76MD *Candid-Bs*, being rather narrower.

The A-50M prototype was built 'green' in 1989 and first flew in March 1990 (presumably this is the first flight after outfitting).

This page:
'50 Red', the last-but-one A-50M (and the last-but-one *Mainstay* for the Soviet PVO), at Ivanovo-Severnyy AB.

Opposite page:
The flight line at Ivanovo-Severnyy AB with four A-50s; the nearest aircraft has no tactical code.

An aerial view of five well-weathered A-50s stored at Ivanovo-Severnyy.

Only six aircraft were built to this standard in 1989-91 in batches 65, 66, 69, 71, 73 and 74, with the tactical codes '44 Red', '45 Red' and '50 Red' through '53 Red' (again allocated randomly). '51 Red' (c/n 1003488634, f/n 6609) was the first *Mainstay* to be shown publicly (at MosAeroShow '92 in Zhukovskiy, Moscow Region) and was the only production example that was not the fifth aircraft in its batch. The A-50M's NATO reporting name is *Mainstay-B*.

In the 21st century the Shmel' mission avionics suite had become obsolescent. Therefore, in the early 2000s the Vega Radio Engineering Corporation (formerly NPO Vega-M) started work on a new mission avionics suite called Shmel'-M. The suite offered   enhanced   detection   capability

The A-50U upgrade prototype, '37 Red', at Kubinka AB where it was demonstrated to the then President of Russia Dmitriy A. Medvedev.

The mission crew workstations of the A-50U feature large LCD screens replacing the old CRT displays, plus new keyboards .

against low-flying targets, determining their coordinates, speed and range (also in an ECM environment); detection range in pursuit mode was also improved. According to some reports, the new suite was able to detect a bomber-sized target at 650 km (404 miles), a fighter-sized target at 300 km (186 miles) and a ground target such as an armoured convoy at 250 km (155 miles). A new satellite navigation (SATNAV) system was introduced, enhancing navigation accuracy. The suite used state-of-the-art electronic components; the CRT displays at the mission crew's workstations gave way to large colour liquid crystal displays (LCDs). The new electronic components not only enhanced reliability but also made the avionics lighter and more compact, giving a sizeable weight saving; this allowed the aircraft to carry more fuel, increasing unrefueled range and endurance. As a bonus, it freed up space in the mission crew cabin,

allowing a galley and a rest area to be provided – a most welcome addition.

The new mid-life upgrade featuring the Shmel'-M suite was designated **A-50U** (*oosovershen*stvovannyy – improved or upgraded). The prototype was converted by TANTK Beriyev from an in-service *Mainstay-A* coded '37 Red' (c/n 0073476298, f/n 5805) in 2004. Outwardly the new version was readily identifiable by the absence of the A-50's signature horizontal strakes – these had been removed, leaving only the root portions which looked like ugly scars on the main gear fairings. (This, incidentally, led to some speculation that the strakes have some other role than stability enhancement, since the upgrade rendered them unnecessary.)

The Shmel'-M suite performed well during trials; the aircraft's flight performance, including field performance, remained unaffected. The trials continued well into 2009; the then Commander-in-Chief of the Russian Air Force Col.-Gen. Aleksandr N. Zelin signed the trials completion report on 26th November that year. This paved the way for further conversions to A-50U standard. On 31st October 2011 the Russian Air Force took delivery of the first 'production' A-50U, '47 Red'/RF-92957 (c/n 0043453577, f/n 4005), also a *Mainstay-A* upgraded in May 2011; it made the type's public debut on 10th August 2012, making a flypast during the Russian Air Force Centennial celebrations at Zhukovskiy. The second 'production' aircraft, '33 Red'/RF-50602 (c/n 0043454618, f/n 4105), made its first post-upgrade flight in late 2012 and was redelivered on 13th April 2013 in an unusual overall dark grey colour scheme; in August 2013 it was displayed statically at the MAKS-2013 airshow in Zhukovskiy. (The

aircraft posing as an A-50U at the MAKS-2011 – '41 Red'/RF-94268 – was in fact an A-50 *sans suffixe*.) In May 2014 this aircraft was christened 'Vladimir Ivanov' to commemorate the former General Director and General Designer of the Vega Radio Engineering Corporation, who died in 1996. Finally, on 25th March 2014 A-50U '37 Red' was also delivered to the Air Force – still minus IFR probe, which had been removed for some reason; it was christened 'Sergey

Atayants' in March and gained the additional quasi-civil registration RF-93966 in early May. Other *Mainstays* are to follow in due course.

Above: '47 Red'/RF-92957, the first production-standard A-50U, was redelivered to the Russian Air Force in 2009. Note the drastically cropped horizontal strakes which are this version's recognition feature.

Below: Unusually, the second production-standard A-50U, '33 Red'/RF-50602, is painted gloss dark grey overall.

Export Aspirations

The A-50 had been first demonstrated to the Indian Air Force as a potential customer as early as February 1984; the aircraft in question was the first production machine, '30 Red'. In the late 1980s the Soviet government agreed to offer the *Mainstay* for export. Hence in 1988 TANTK Beriyev converted a single A-50 ('46 Red', '38 Red' or '34 Red') into the prototype of an export version designated **A-50E** (**eks**portnyy – export, used attributively), or *izdeliye* AE. In fact, the conversion boiled down to the removal of certain avionics not intended for export and to installation of additional wall trim panels in the mission crew cabin. The A-50E was demonstrated to Admiral Jayant Ganpat Nadkarni, Chairman of India's Joint Chiefs of Staff, at Kubinka AB west of Moscow in 1988, but the aircraft was found to be incompatible with India's existing air defence system, and no Indian Air Force order ensued. The unwanted A-50E sat idle for a long time, diverting human resources for maintenance, until it was reconverted to standard configuration and returned to the PVO.

Interestingly, the A-50E designation was dusted off in the early 2000 when TANTK Beriyev showed a model marked as such at one of the biennial Hydro Aviation Shows at Ghelendjik on the Black Sea. The model featured PS-90A-76 turbofans but retained the standard rotodome. The aircraft did not materialise in this guise – but see the A-50EI section below.

The next try was in 1994, when India's geopolitical rival, China, started negotiations with Russian and Western avionics manufacturers on the conversion of the *Candid* into an AWACS for the People's Liberation Army Air Force (PLAAF). The British company GEC-Marconi offered the Argus

2000 mechanically scanned radar system (as fitted to the unsuccessful British Aerospace Nimrod AEW Mk.1) but lost out to Elta Electronics, a division of Israel Aircraft Industries (IAI), which offered a more sophisticated mission avionics suite built around the EL/M-2075 Phalcon surveillance radar. Phalcon is an acronym for PHased-Array L-band CONformal [Radar]; 'L-band' means an operating frequency of 1-2 GHz and a wavelength of 30-15 cm (11^{13}⁄$_{16}$ in to 5^{29}⁄$_{32}$ in). Interestingly, China was adamant that it would not buy the Phalcon system unless it was installed on the Il-76.

It took a lot of persuasion before the Russian government authorised the sale of an A-50 to Israel, which was certainly not among the traditional buyers of Russian military hardware. Some sources suggest Russia was reluctant to supply a *Mainstay* to IAI for conversion because it had hoped to sell the A-50 to China in 'as-was' condition. Eventually, however, permission was granted. On 17th June 1997 the Rosvo'oruzheniye (= Russian Weapons) arms export agency and TANTK Beriyev inked a deal with IAI at the 42nd Paris Air Show covering the installation of the Phalcon radar in the A-50's airframe – the first military technology deal between Russia and Israel. The resulting combination was known as the **A-50I** or *izdeliye* AI, the I standing for *izrail'skoye* [*oboroodovaniye*] – Israeli equipment. The contract was signed by Rosvo'oruzheniye General Director Aleksandr I. Kotyolkin, TANTK Beriyev General Designer Ghennadiy S. Panatov and IAI President Moshe Keret.

Originally the antenna arrays were to be housed in bulbous radomes on the nose, the tailcone and the forward fuselage sides (in similar fashion to IAI's Boeing 707-320 AWACS equipped with the Phalcon radar), and the result looked really bizarre. However, this arrangement was soon discarded in favour of the then-latest EL/W-2090 radar (a derivative of the EL/M-2075 and EL/W-2085) housed in a conventional rotodome carried on twin pylons. Actually the word 'rotodome' is not applicable in this case – the lentil-shaped structure was in fact *fixed*; its metal centre portion was an equilateral triangle mounting three active electronically scanned array (AESA) antennas, each covering a sector of 120°; accordingly, there were three dielectric portions instead of two. The 'unrotodome' had a slightly larger diameter – 11.5 m (37 ft 8¾ in) versus 10.8 m on the A-50/A-50M – and the pylons had constant chord instead of tapering towards the top. The entire structure together with the pylons weighed about 13 tons (28,660 lb).

Below: This model marked A-50E was displayed at one of the Hydro Aviation Shows at Ghelendjik, showing a proposed export version with PS-90A-76 engines but with a conventional rotodome.

Opposite page:
The as-yet unmarked A-50I takes off from Taganrog-Yoozhnyy on its first flight on 28th July 1999.

This air-to-air shot of the A-50I shows the fixed 'unrotodome' with a triangular centre portion and three dielectric sections. Note the still-unpainted ventral fins and wingtips and the plainly visible overpainted star insignia on the wings.

The triangular horizontal strakes on the main gear fairings characteristic of the *Mainstay-A/B* were deleted; instead, the A-50I had twin splayed trapezoidal ventral fins under the rear fuselage to enhance directional stability. The cooling air intake at the base of the fin, another trademark feature of the standard *Mainstay*, was also omitted, as were the dielectric panel immediately below the rudder (only the dielectric tailcone remained) and the large ECM blisters on the fuselage sides; the ECM antennas were relocated to the suitably redesigned wingtip fairings. On the other hand, there were a few blade aerials which the standard A-50 did not have. Incidentally, the A-50I carried a total of 71 miscellaneous antennas and aerials, 44 of which were associated with the

Here the A-50I is shown in a later test flight, wearing a fresh coat of paint and the Russian flag but no registration as yet. Note that the original A-50M's horizontal strakes have been removed completely – unlike those of the A-50U.

AWACS suite. Finally, the front end of the port main gear fairing had the usual shape (typical of the *Mainstay*, that is) but featured only the larger of the two cooling air intakes; there were two intakes on the starboard side.

The IFR probe was retained, since the aircraft was supposed to work with the PLAAF's Xian HU-6 and H-6DU hose-and-drogue tankers derived from the H-6 bomber (licence-built Tupolev Tu-16 *Badger*). Changes were made to the electrics, the mission equipment cooling system, the oxygen system and so on.

The interior layout was revised to feature a mission crew compartment with ten operator workstations and a rest area with nine seats and utility equipment – an important bonus made possible by the more compact Israeli avionics. The aircraft had a flight crew of five, a mission crew of ten and a relief crew of nine. A noise suppression bulkhead separated the crew section from the rest of the cabin. An escape hatch was provided, enabling the mission crew to bail out via the cargo ramp.

In Russia the development of the A-50I was supervised by Ye. P. Konstantinov, with I. V. Kalinin heading the actual design effort. Despite all the previous experience with the *Mainstay*, the A-50I programme necessitated a large scope of research and development work, including wind tunnel tests at TsAGI and a series of static and resonance frequency tests. The latter tests were performed on a specially manufactured Il-76 fuselage section mated to the pylons and the 'saucer' radome.

Unique know-how was evolved in the course of this programme. For the first time in Russian aircraft design practice TANTK Beriyev made use of computer-aided design (CAD) software to create a 3-D model of the radome and arrange the equipment inside it. This made it possible to integrate the equipment properly, calculate the required length of the wiring runs and check out the ease of maintenance access. It would have been

impossible to observe the tight development schedule set forth in the contract if a traditional wooden mock-up had been constructed.

The next stage was the actual prototype construction, which again proceeded in accordance with the tight schedule stipulated by the contract. To achieve this, TANTK Beriyev had to enlist the assistance of numerous subcontractors; in some high-priority areas the work went ahead in 24/7 mode.

The A-50M prototype, '44 Red' (c/n 0093486579, f/n 6505), was transferred from the Russian Air Force for conversion as the A-50I prototype. Stripped of the Shmel' mission avionics suite and incorporating appropriate structural changes, the aircraft made its uneventful first flight as the A-50I from Taganrog-Yoozhnyy on 28th July 1999, piloted by a crew comprising captain Ghennadiy G. Kalyuzhnyy, co-pilot Konstantin V. Babich, navigator Yu. N. Gherasimov, flight engineer V. A. Chebanov and test engineer B. G. Dikoon.

The manufacturer's tests included 15 test flights and seven training flights. At that point the A-50I wore no markings except a Russian flag on the fin; on 26th October 1999 the aircraft was registered RA-78740, making the delivery flight to Tel Aviv-Ben Gurion airport that same day. Shortly afterwards it was placed on the Israeli register as 4X-AGI.

The cost of outfitting a *Mainstay* to A-50I standard (not counting the aircraft itself) was estimated at US$ 250 million. Apart from the radar, the aircraft was to feature a signals intelligence (SIGINT) system capable of eavesdropping on enemy communications and pinpointing the location of enemy radars in the battle area.

RA-78740 was to be the first of four A-50Is ordered by the PLAAF. However, despite being on reasonably good terms with China, the USA saw the A-50I deal as a threat to Taiwan (which Beijing purportedly still aims to recapture by force) and began putting pressure on Israel, trying to stop the deal from coming through. Israel put on a show of defiance at first (the then Prime Minister Ehud Barak said IAI would fulfil its contract obligations no matter what) but gave in when the USA threatened to withdraw US$ 20 billion worth of military aid. Barak lost the 2001 elections, and the new Prime Minister Ariel Sharon cancelled the A-50I deal shortly afterwards. Still, this was not the end of the Chinese AWACS story (see below).

Now, let's turn our attention to India again. In 1999, following an abortive attempt to create an indigenous AWACS based on the Il-76MD (the Airborne Surveillance Platform radar technology testbed converted from a HAL 748-224 Srs 2 twin-turboprop transport crashed before a proper prototype could be built), the Indian Air Force sized up the *Mainstay* once again. First, when the then Vice Prime Minister of Russia Il'ya I. Klebanov visited New Delhi in December 1999, an agreement was signed envisaging a short-term lease of a single A-50 to the IAF. The aircraft arrived at Chandigarh AB, Punjab, in April 2000. During the lease it made ten sorties lasting up to six hours each; it was piloted by a Russian Air Force crew but a number of IAF specialists were also on board.

The experience gained during this evaluation was generally positive. After a period of negotiations, in 2003 India placed a US$500 million order with Russia for three *Mainstays* tailored to IAF requirements – specifically, more capable mission avionics and a more advanced powerplant. The first of the three aircraft was due for delivery in June 2007; the flyaway price was estimated at US$350 million.

Designated **A-50EI** (**eks**portnyy, in**deey**skiy – export, Indian), the new export version again featured an Elta Electronics EL/W-2090 AESA radar capable of logging 60 targets simultaneously from a range of 400 km (248 miles). The mission avionics suites for the three aircraft were ordered under a separate Indian-Israeli US$ 1.1 billion contract signed in March 2004. Another fundamental difference is that the A-50EI was powered by Aviadvigatel' (Solov'yov) PS-90A-76 turbofans rated at 14,500 kgp (31,970 lbst), which had first found use on the *Candid* family when the stretched Il-76MF military transport flew in 1995. Although this reduces spares commonality with the IAF's fleet of Il-76MD transports in service since 1985, the new engines are more powerful and fuel-efficient.

Outwardly the new export version was similar to the ill-starred A-50I, featuring the same fixed 'unrotodome' with three dielectric portions and constant-chord pylons, the same rear end treatment (with canted ventral fins, no cooling air intake and one rear dielectric fairing) and the same wingtip-mounted ECM antennas. The main external difference was in the engines, which were housed in fatter nacelles tapering towards the rear. Another different feature was the dorsal SATCOM antenna fairing which was shorter and more convex – almost hemispherical – instead of having a flattened teardrop shape.

The contract was finalised in early 2005. The first of the three aircraft (IAF serials KW-3551 through KW-3553, f/ns 9402 through 9404) was manufactured 'green' by TAPO and delivered to TANTK for conversion in 2005, making its first post-conversion

KW-3552, the second production A-50EI, at Taganrog-Yoozhnyy during pre-delivery tests, with an attendant APA-100 GPU on a Ural-4320 chassis. The larger nacelles of the PS-90A-76 engines are clearly visible.

A-50EI KW-3552 in a pre-delivery test flight, showing the wingtip ECM fairings and the dorsal SATCOM blister. The aircraft wears its Indian Air Force serial but not the IAF roundels and fin flash; all doors and hatches are heavily outlined.

flight at Taganrog-Yoozhnyy on 29th November 2007; on 20th January 2008 it was flown to Tel Aviv-Ben Gurion for outfitting. On 25th May 2009, two years later than anticipated, KW-3551 arrived at Jamnagar AB, Gujarat; the official handover ceremony took place one day later at Palam AB near New Delhi. The other two aircraft followed in 2010 and 2011. At present the three A-50EIs are in service with the aptly designated 50 Sqn at Agra, Uttar-Pradesh, established in 2010. In April 2010 India requested a proposal from IAI to supply another three A-50EIs. Unfortunately TAPO has ceased aircraft production, having been driven into bankruptcy by the Uzbekistan government; however, a number of unfinished Il-76 airframes remains at the factory, and an agreement has been reached to deliver at least two of them (f/ns 9405 and 9409) by road and river to Taganrog, where they will be completed as A-50EIs.

Left and below:
Here, KW-3552 makes a practice refuelling from a Russian Air Force IL-78 *sans suffixe* tanker, '33 Blue'.

Bottom: Seen from the refuelling systems operator's station of the IL-78, A-50EI KW-3552 leaves contrails across the sky as it flies over the countryside of southern Russia during tests.

'Friends and Relatives'

It is worth noting here that the A-50 has a couple of more distant 'relatives'. Firstly, the Iraqi Air Force – the first (and largest) foreign customer for the Il-76 developed several versions of the Il-76 on its own initiative, including airborne early warning variants. Interestingly, the last 15 Il-76MDs delivered to the IrAF were built with no gunner's station and may thus be termed as Il-76MD 'Falsies'. In 1988 one of these (identity unknown) was converted into an AWACS aircraft known as **Baghdad-1**. A Thomson-CSF TRS-2100 Tigre S surveillance radar manufactured locally under French licence was installed under the rear fuselage in a huge GRP radome supplanting the cargo doors, with a strake below it to improve directional stability. Like most IrAF *Candids*, the aircraft wore Iraqi Airways livery but the logos and registration were painted out. Iraqi specialists claimed that the radar, which was manned by four operators, had a scan 'substantially in excess of 180°' and could detect, identify and track targets at up to 350 km (190 nm) range. Since in its basic form the Tigre is ground-based, changes were made to the radar set in order to reduce susceptibility to ground clutter. Tactical information was transmitted in real time by data link or voice link; the aircraft also featured indigenous radio and radar ESM equipment.

However, the unconventionally located antenna had a limited scan and was extremely vulnerable to tailstrike on take-off and landing. Therefore, two more Il-76MD 'Falsies' were converted later for the AWACS role as the **Adnan-1** and **Adnan-2** (named after former Iraqi Defence Minister Gen. Adnan Khajrallah Talfah killed in a helicopter crash in May 1988). These had a Thomson-CSF TRS-2105/06 Tigre G radar installed in a conventional rotodome of 9 m (29 ft 6 in) diameter mounted on twin pylons immediately aft of the wings. Two canted trapezoidal strakes were fitted to the rear fuselage to ensure directional stability; these

were smaller and placed higher than those of the A-50I/A-50EI. The first aircraft had a grey/white colour scheme but no insignia other than an Iraqi flag and 'Adnan-1' titles in Arabic, whereas the Adnan-2 wore full IrAF insignia and two-tone grey wraparound camouflage.

All three Iraqi AWACS conversions were used operationally in 1990 during the First Gulf War (the Iraqi invasion of Kuwait and the ensuing Operation *Desert Storm* to expel Iraqi troops from Kuwait). In so doing the Adnan-2 AWACS was destroyed on the ground by an anti-Iraqi coalition force air strike. When Saddam Hussein realised he was losing the war, the Baghdad-1 and Adnan-1 AWACS were flown to neighbouring Iran in January 1991 along with other Iraqi aircraft to escape destruction by the Allies. However, the Iranians took advantage of this windfall, interning the aircraft (since Iran maintained a neutral stance in the war) and subsequently appropriating them as reparations for damages sustained in the preceding Iran-Iraq War of 1980-88.

In Iran the Baghdad-1 received the Islamic Republic of Iran Air Force (IRIAF) serial 5-8206 but was probably never used operationally, sitting in storage at Tehran-Mehrabad International airport in rather tatty condition. Conversely, the Adnan-1, which was renamed **'Simorgh'** (a benevolent flying creature with magical properties from Persian mythology), remained operational as IRIAF 5-8208. According to some sources, the original Tigre G radar was replaced with a newer Iranian-made radar, which could trace aerial targets within a 1,000-km (621-mile) range, and the upgrade was performed with Russian assistance. The aircraft entered service in April 2008; however, its career proved to be brief. On 22nd September 2009 the Simorgh AWACS crashed during a military parade marking the 29th anniversary of the start of the Iran-Iraq War; it featured a flypast of several IRIAF aircraft. Some sources claim that a fire broke out in one of the

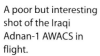

A poor but interesting shot of the Iraqi Adnan-1 AWACS in flight.

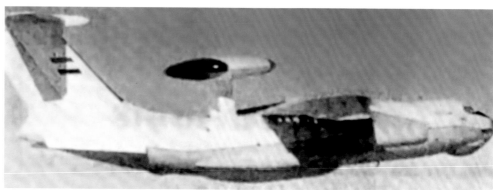

Escorted by two Iraqi Air Force MiG-29 fighters, the Adnan-1 makes a flypast over Baghdad during a military parade in 1991.

Il-76MD's engines; the crew attempted an emergency landing on runway 29L at Mehrabad International airport but the rotodome broke away (possibly as a result of the pylons being overstressed in an excessively vigorous manoeuvre) and struck the tail unit, severing it from the airframe. Other sources suggest that there was a mid-air collision with an escorting Northrop F-5F Tiger II fighter serialled 3-7167 whose crew of two ejected and survived. Whatever the cause, the tailless Il-76MD crashed out of control 15 km (9.3 miles) northwest of the city of Varamin (Tehran Province), killing the crew of seven.

Now, let's turn our attention to China once again. What became of the one-off

Here the former Adnan-1 is seen in Islamic Republic of Iran Air Force markings as the Simorgh, with the serial 5-8208 in Farsi on the nose.

Another shot of the Simorgh on the runway at Tehran-Mehrabad International airport where it was based.

A rather crude model of the KJ-2000 AWACS at Airshow China in Zhuhai.

A-50I, you may ask? Israel's pullout from the programme did not upset China's plans completely. Research Institute No.14 in Nanjing (aka NETRI – Nanjing Electronic Technology Research Institute) was tasked with developing an indigenous phased-array radar that would fit into the A-50I's existing radome. The result was a Sino-Russian AWACS designated **KJ-2000** (KJ stands for *Kong Jing* – 'Sky Guard'). Wang Xiaomo was the chief project engineer, with Bai Shucheng responsible for the design of the 'unrotodome'; development of the radar at NETRI was supervised by Wu Manqing.

Stripped of mission avionics, the A-50I was eventually delivered to China on 10th June 2002 as RA-78740. In 2002-03 it was outfitted with a new mission equipment suite at the Xian Aircraft Co. (XAC) plant, making its first post-conversion flight on 11th November 2003. The aircraft was taken on strength by the China Flight Test Estab-

'762 Black', the KJ-2000 prototype, at Xian-Yanliang AB.

lishment (CFTE) at Xian (Yanliang AB) and serialled '762 Black', with appropriate titles in Chinese and English. When its existence became known to the West, the KJ-2000 received a separate NATO reporting name, *Mainring*.

Next thing, the China Aviation Technology Industries Corp. (CATIC) purchased a high-time Il-76MD, 76579, from the Ukrainian Air Force in late 2002. This aircraft was turned over to the First Aircraft Institute in Xian and converted into a static test airframe for the KJ-2000. The tail gunner's station was retained in so doing, making it the sole *Mainring* to have one. Apparently the airframe was not tested to destruction and is currently preserved in Xian not far from Yanliang AB. A further high-time airframe, Il-76T RA-76458, was acquired from Russia in 2000, and this was likewise converted to a ground test article for the KJ-2000, with 'YH2000' titles applied.

Another view of the prototype flying in the vicinity of Xian, showing the CFTE titles (in Chinese and English) and logo.

Still wearing its original quasi-civil registration B-4043, the second 'production' KJ-2000 is seen at Xian-Yanliang during pre-delivery tests; it was serialled '30074 Red' upon delivery. The modified parts of the airframe are still in primer.

At the time the PLAAF operated 14 quasi-civil Il-76MD 'Falsies' in the colours of its commercial division, China United Airlines. Four of these were progressively converted to KJ-2000s by XAC; the first of these was B-4040, which made its first post-conversion flight in April 2004, followed by B-4043, B-4041 and B-4042. While most of the external features had been copied from the prototype, there were differences. Thus, the 'production' KJ-2000s retained the port side entry door but lacked the IFR probe; the weather radar's radome was almost identical to the Il-76's, the ESM antenna fairing below it lacked the distinctive tooth-like projections seen on the A-50, while the dorsal SAT-COM blister had a strongly convex shape similar to that of the A-50EI. The front ends of the main gear fairings retained the standard shape typical of the Il-76 and the TA-6 APU remained at its usual position, with a lateral exhaust ahead of the port forward main gear strut, although the air intake door had been deleted (each fairing featured one large circular air intake for a heat exchanger and a lateral outlet grille, the port intake serving the APU as well). Moreover, a turbine

generator unit was added at the rear end of the port fairing, breathing through an 'elephant's ear' air intake (which had a different shape from that on the A-50); the exhaust was located laterally, not ventrally, and had a larger diameter than the APU exhaust. The four aircraft gained a bluish grey colour scheme with pale grey undersurfaces, initially retaining their civil registrations; later they received full military markings with the PLAAF serials 30071 Red through 30074 Red. The KJ-2000s are in service with the 26th Special Mission Air Division/76th Regiment at Wuxi (Shuofang AB).

While we are on the subject of the A-50, mention should be made of a Soviet aircraft which was developed by the same OKBs (Il'yushin and Beriyev) and is rather similar externally but fills a quite different role (which is why it is in this section of the book). Monitoring and recording systems operation during test launches of ballistic and cruise missiles is something of a problem, since conventional data recorders are highly unlikely to be retrieved intact when the missile drops – or blows up. The only reliable method is to transmit systems data by means of telemetry

This page:
KJ-2000 '30072 Red' in full PLAAF insignia in service with the 26th Special Mission Air Division/76th Regiment.

The same aircraft escorted by Chengdu J-7G fighters during a rehearsal for a flypast.

Opposite page:
Escorted by J-7GB fighters of the PLAAF's '1st August' aerobatic team, KJ-2000 '30072 Red' passes over Tiananmen Square in Beijing on 1st October 2009 during the grand parade on occasion of the People's Republic of China 60th anniversary.

This view of '30072 Red' shows well the KJ-2000's modified nose, the extra turbine power unit in the rear portion of the port main gear fairing, the dorsal SATCOM blister, the ventral fins and the tail radome. Note the red reference stripes used by the pilots of the escorting fighters for formation-keeping during the parade.

which is picked up by ground stations or specially equipped aircraft.

Initially the Flight Research Institute named after Mikhail M. Gromov (LII – **Lyot**no-is**sled**ovatel'skiy insti**toot**) used the Il-18SIP (samo**lyot**nyy izme**rit**el'nyy poonkt – airborne measuring station) based on the Il-18A four-turboprop airliner. When the Il-18SIP (CCCP-27220) had to be retired in due course, LII had to find a replacement. First, two *Candid-B*s (Il-76 *sans suffixe* CCCP-86721 and Il-76M CCCP-86024) were converted into almost identical telemetry pickup aircraft known as 'aircraft 676' and

'aircraft 776' respectively. These shared some of the equipment with the Il-18SIP and its new-build production version, the Il-20RT (*retranslyator* – relay aircraft).

Operational experience with 'aircraft 676' and 'aircraft 776' led to the development of a specialised radar picket version of the Il-76MD designated **'aircraft 976'** or **SKIP** (*samolyotnyy komahndno-izmeritel'nyy poonkt* – airborne measuring and control station, AMCS). The unusual designation is probably derived from the aircraft's product code which could be *izdeliye* 976. Development was completed in the mid-1980s. Since the aircraft was again

This plan view of a KJ-2000 shows clearly the design of the fixed 'unrotodome' with three dielectric portions and the wingtip ECM fairings. All engine cowlings are open for maintenance.

A KJ-2000 parked under one of the shelters at Wuxi (Shuofang AB) preventing observation by US surveillance satellites.

KJ-2000 '30074 Red' in (mostly) primer finish after the conversion.

Above: The same aircraft in full PLAAF colours. The formation-keeping stripes suggest the aircraft was a back-up for '30072 Red' during the 60th anniversary parade.

Below: A fine sunset shot of KJ-2000 '30071 Red' on final approach to Wuxi-Shuofang.

Right and below:
The first of five 'aircraft 976', CCCP-76452, makes a low flypast at Zhukovskiy in the late 1980s. The aircraft was quite new at the time.

developed jointly with TANTK Beriyev, it has been erroneously referred to in the West as 'Be-976'.

The aircraft was superficially similar to the A-50, featuring an identical RA-10 rotodome – which, incidentally, earned it the nickname *Pogahnka* (Toadstool) at LII. Like the A-50, it had a SATCOM antenna fairing ahead of the wings and two ventral strake aerials aft of the nose gear.

But here the similarity ended. 'Aircraft 976' retained the standard navigator's station glazing, the tail gunner's station (used as an equipment operator's station), the cargo doors and the port side entry door; there was no IFR probe. The main gear fairings and APU location were likewise unchanged as compared to the Il-76MD, and the A-50's characteristic horizontal strakes were missing – probably because the mission equipment was different, hence the weight distribution was also different and the rotodome did not have such a drastic effect on longitudinal stability. The UKU-9K-502 cannon barbette was replaced

by a hemispherical radome which was larger than the A-50's rear dielectric fairing (but shorter and more bulbous than the rear 'thimble' radome of 'aircraft 676'/'aircraft 776'), and the PRS-4 *Box Tail* gun ranging radar above the gunner's station was deleted. Two massive cylindrical equipment pods were installed at the wingtips, carrying the navigation lights; their front and rear portions were dielectric, enclosing flat-plate antennas. As on 'aircraft 676' and 'aircraft 776', four long probe aerials were located around the navigator's station. Three L-shaped aerials were mounted on each side of the fin; four L-shaped aerials of a different type were mounted ahead of the flight deck windscreen, the inner ones facing forward and the outer ones aft; several additional blade aerials were fitted under the main gear fairings. The freight hold was crammed with data processing and storage equipment; this was modular, allowing the aircraft to be reconfigured for specific missions (part of it could be mounted on the cargo ramp).

Five new Il-76MDs built in 1986-87 were converted to 'aircraft 976' standard. Despite their near-military role, they wore the 1973-standard blue/white livery of Aeroflot Soviet Airlines (just like Soviet Air Force Il-76s) and were registered CCCP-76452 through CCCP-76456 (although they were not manufactured consecutively); three out of five aircraft still wore the Soviet prefix and flag in the 2000s. The only deviation from the standard livery is that the nose titles read '976' instead of 'Il-76MD' and the flag was carried higher on the tail than usual.

The AMCS were used to monitor the trajectories and systems status of manned and unmanned aerial and space vehicles in real time. Unmanned aerial vehicles (UAVs) could be remote-controlled; a self-destruct command could be transmitted if an experimental missile went haywire and headed where it shouldn't. Telemetry data was processed, taped and transmitted in real time to ground control and telemetry processing centres by radio or satellite link, thus obviating the need to build additional facilities in remote areas. Tracking range was 1,000 km (621 miles) and trajectories are measured with an accuracy of 30 m (98 ft). The six telemetry chan-

nels had a data transfer rate of 2 million baud (2 Mb per second). Endurance was 8 hours.

'Aircraft 976' participated in the trials of the Tupolev Tu-160 *Blackjack* strategic missile carrier, monitoring test launches of Raduga Kh-55M (AS-15 *Kent*) cruise missiles. LII claimed the AMCS may also be used for ecological monitoring 'and other purposes' (*sic*).

The existence of 'aircraft 976' was revealed on 16th August 1988 during the Aviation Day flypast in Zhukovskiy. Since the A-50 had been sighted in 1987, of course Western journalists believed the 'toadstools' to be prototypes of the A-50; it was some time before the matter was clarified. Nevertheless, 'aircraft 976' received the reporting name *Mainstay-C*.

Starting with MosAeroShow '92 in August 1992, 'aircraft 976' has been a regular participant at the Moscow airshows in Zhukovskiy; all five examples have been in the static display at some time or other. However, in the 2000s the AMCS sat idle most of the time due to the dire situation in the Russian aerospace industry and the lull in missile tests; apparently only two aircraft

Above and left: 'Aircraft 976' CCCP-76453 in the static park of the MosAeroShow '92 airshow at Zhukovskiy. The wingtip pods, the tail radome and the triple L-shaped aerials on the fin are clearly visible. Note the tell-tale wear and tear on the rotodome, which was originally light grey.

This aspect of an 'aircraft 976' shows the standard IL-76 nose glazing and main gear fairings. Note the array of probe aerials on the nose which is another recognition feature of this version.

(RA-76453 and 76455 – the latter had the nationality prefix removed, being placed on the Russian experimental aircraft register) remained active. There were plans to use the 'aircraft 976' in conjunction with the Burlak suborbital launch vehicle programme (the vehicle was to be carried aloft and launched by the suitably modified Tu-160SK), but the project did not materialise.

Since the aircraft were low-time air-frames, a decision was taken to convert them for other uses. Thus, in early 2004 CCCP-76456 was converted into an engine testbed broadly similar to LII's own Il-76LL testbeds and sold to China. This involved removing the rotodome and associated pylons, the lower pair of nose probes and some of the additional aerials, replacing the No.2 (port inboard) D-30KP engine with a special pod housing the experimental engine and installing test equipment heat exchangers in characteristic fairings on the fuselage sides immediately aft of the wings. After a period of preliminary flight tests at LII (still registered 76456) in 2005 the aircraft was delivered to the CFTE, where it is currently operated as '760 Black'. In 2007 'aircraft 976' CCCP-76454 was similarly converted into Il-76LL 76454 and operated by LII and the PowerJet consortium (a Russian-French joint venture between the engine maker NPO Saturn and the Safran Group) as a testbed for the SaM 146 turbofan developed for the Sukhoi Superjet 100 regional airliner. In this case, the wingtip pods and all non-standard aerials were removed as well.

In due course the second 'aircraft 976' was placed on the Russian registers as RA-76453, gaining the Russian flag and the logo of its operator, LII, on the nose. The flag is located higher than usual because of the tail aerials.

An interesting aspect of two 'aircraft 976' in old and new markings on the south side of the LII airfield in Zhukovskiy.

A fine study of 'aircraft 976' 76455 flying over Zhukovskiy. The aircraft wears the Russian flag but no prefix, being placed on the experimental aircraft register. On reflection, it could use a fresh coat of paint…

A display model of 'aircraft 976' RA-76453 with 'IL-76SK' nose titles displayed at one of the MAKS airshows.

The Shape of Things to Come

In 2000 the Il'yushin OKB proposed an AWACS aircraft based on the Il-76MD-90 (a version of the Il-76MD re-engined with PS-90A-76 turbofans) and tentatively designated **Il-150**. This indicates that the aircraft was basically a PS-90 powered A-50 – a follow-on to the A-50M as originally projected, and perhaps a stepping stone towards the A-50EI.

As mentioned earlier, the TAPO factory in Tashkent was being purposely driven into bankruptcy by a corrupt government which would not let the factory sign contracts and sell its aircraft. Hence TAPO was unable to complete several important orders, including an order for a large batch of Il-76MDs and Il-78 *Midas* tankers for China. Therefore, in 2006 the Russian United Aircraft Corporation (UAC) took the decision to transfer Il-76 production to Russia – specifically, to the Aviastar-SP plant in Ul'yanovsk, which was short of work (production of the Antonov An-124 Ruslan/*Condor* heavy transport had ended and attempts to relaunch it were getting nowhere, while the upgraded Tu-204SM airliner was facing an uncertain future). The Il'yushin Aircraft Complex took this opportunity to undertake a thorough upgrade of the transport, bringing out the Il-76MD-90A

powered by PS-90A-76 engines. As compared to the identically powered Il-76MD-90 mid-life upgrade which has been undergoing tests since December 2005, the new-build Il-76MD-90A (the A stands for Aviastar), or *izdeliye* 476, has a considerably redesigned wing structure with fewer production breaks, a new navigation suite and a new 'glass cockpit' with six liquid-crystal displays. The prototype was completed in December 2011 and made its first flight from Ul'yanovsk-Vostochnyy (= Ul'yanovsk-East) on 22nd September 2012.

Accordingly the Il-76MD-90A was chosen as the platform for the Russian Air Force's next-generation AWACS, which is designated **A-100** (a hint at being 'twice as capable as the A-50'?) or *izdeliye* PM and has the popular name *Prem'yer* (Premier, or Prime Minister… good grief!). The information available on this project so far is rather sketchy and somewhat contradictory. Most sources report that the Vega Radio Engineering Corporation is responsible for the A-100's mission avionics suite (which is built around the Prem'yer radar) and that the company favours a conventional rotodome with the radar beam being scanned mechanically in azimuth and electronically in elevation. Photos of a display model in Aviastar-SP house colours do not give a clear idea of the rotodome type. Another desktop model of the A-100 (in Russian Air Force grey colours) shown in February 2014 does indeed have a *Mainstay-A/B/C* style conventional rotodome; this is reportedly to turn at 12 rpm – twice the speed of the A-50's rotodome. The model also features dielectric fairings for ECM/ESM antennas on the flight deck roof, ahead of the main gear fairings and below the rudder. There have been claims, however, that the Vega Radio Engineering Corporation turned down the job, and that the rival Research Institute of Instrument Engineering named after Viktor V. Tikhomirov (NIIP – *Naoochno-issledovatel'skiy institoot priborostroyeniya*), which took on the job, is developing an AESA radar in a fixed 'unrotodome' similar to that of the A-50EI.

The A-100 prototype is reported to be under construction at TANTK Beriyev in 2014, using one of the A-50 airframes stored at Taganrog-Yoozhnyy. This is a stop-gap measure meant to save time because no Il-76MD-90A is available for conversion; subsequent A-100s will be new-build airframes. The first flight was originally expected to take place in 2015, but has now been postponed until 2016. There are no plans to build an export version.

A display model of the A-100 AWACS in Aviastar-SP house colours at one of the international airshows. Note the '*izdeliye* 476' nose titles applying to the AWACS platform (the IL-76MD-90A transport), not to the A-100 as such.

A different model of the A-100 with the TANTK Beriyev logo on the base. It represents a later configuration with additional forward, aft and lateral ESM fairings. The rotodome is clearly a conventional one.

The A-50 In Service

Until 1990 the A-50s flew primarily routine training missions, periodically participating in major Soviet Armed Forces or joint Warsaw Pact exercises. Initially the 67th IAEWS operated from the base near Siauliai which had hosted the Tu-126; in 1991, however, this base had to be vacated for political reasons. The *Mainstays* moved north to Beryozovka AB near Pechora on the Kola Peninsula (which the crews were very unhappy about), serving with a new unit – the 144th OAP DRLO (*otdel'nyy aviapolk dahl'nevo rahdiolokatsionnovo obnaruzheniya* – Independent AEW Regiment). A-50s were also detached to the Far East Military District (MD) and to the Crimea Peninsula, operating from Black Sea Fleet airbases and checking on the Soviet Union's southern borders in practice missions. Several aircraft were deployed to Ukurey AB in the Transbaikalian MD, which was home to the 192nd Military Airlift Regiment equipped with Il-76MDs.

In 1997 the PVO ceased to exist as a separate branch of the Armed Forces, being merged into the Russian Air Force (VVS – *Voyenno-vozdooshnyye seely*); thus, for the first time the A-50s came under VVS control. In the autumn of 1998 an AEW&C Aircraft Combat Application Unit was established at Ivanovo-Severnyy AB (= Ivanovo-North), with Col. Sergey A. Konovalov as the unit's first CO. Henceforth most of the operational *Mainstays* were concentrated at this base – which, incidentally, again hosts large numbers of Il-76M/MDs, facilitating logistics and maintenance issues.

The A-50 may operate in patrol mode (loitering over a designated area), on-call mode (being summoned from stand-by alert on the ground or in the air) or escort mode (supporting the actions of a large aircraft group). It may work with ground or shipboard command centres as an additional source of information, or as the main one if there is no alternative radar coverage. In a typical mission the aircraft loiters at about 10,000 m (32,800 ft) on a figure-eight course with 100 km (62 miles) between the centres of the two orbits. The radar displays show targets marked as 'friendly', 'identity unknown' or 'hostile'; 'friendly' aircraft blips are accompanied by the aircraft's tactical code or callsign and information on speed, altitude, heading and fuel status. The mission crew chief coordinates the crew's actions and communicates with C^3I centres. The ROs monitor the tactical situation, tracking aerial and maritime targets, and make adjustments to the automatic acquisition/tracking and IFF systems, acquiring and identifying targets manually if necessary. The RIOs direct interceptors and tactical aircraft towards their targets, working with ground

A-50 *sans suffixe* '46 Red' is towed from its hardstand at Ivanovo-Severnyy AB by a MAZ-537 prime mover.

A-50 '47 Red' takes off at Ivanovo-Severnyy AB, with two sister ships in the background.

An A-50 with the IFR probe removed flies over the rolling hills of the Ashuluk practice range near Astrakhan', southern Russia, during one of the annual PVO exercises.

This view shows how the A-50's 'upper deck' can be accessed and a ladder hooked up for maintenance access to the rotodome's interior via a hatch in the metal centre portion.

Left and below:
A-50s were often deployed to Russia's northern bases to monitor the northern regions and interact with tactical and strategic aircraft during exercises. A-50M '45 Red' is pictured during one of these deployments.

A-50M '51 Red' tucks up its landing gear on take-off from Ivanovo-Severnyy AB. It is the only known example to wear the badge of the locally-based AEW&C unit on both sides.

The *Mainstays* ranged far and wide during exercises. Here A-50M '51 Red' is seen flying over the snow-covered Himalayas.

The early version of the badge of the 2457th AEW&C Unit based at Ivanovo, featuring an owl over the globe and the acronym SRLDN (*samolyot rahdiolokatsionnovo dozora i navedeniya* – AEW&C aircraft). Normally the A-50 wears this badge on the starboard side only.

A-50M '51 Red' made the type's public debut at the MosAeroShow '92 in Zhukovskiy in August 1992. The aircraft was pristine at the time and wore no unit insignia. Note the deployed thrust reversers on all four engines.

Opposite page:
Here, the same aircraft is seen at a PLAAF airbase during one of the annual Sino-Russian *Peace Mission* exercises. Note that the ground power unit is Chinese but the AK-1.6-9A articulated air conditioning units towed by KamAZ-5410 tractors are Russian, having been airlifted to the base for the occasion.

With an APA-5D GPU on an Ural-4320 chassis providing ground power, '51 Red' stands on ready alert.

Lit by the setting sun, A-50M '51 Red' looks impressive as it sits on a snowbound apron at Ivanovo.

command centres or autonomously (if there are no ground-based control assets). In the former case orders are received from ground command centres via secure voice link; in the latter case the aircraft are given orders to attack at the discretion of the RIOs. A combination of both modes is also possible when the A-50 controls the actions of a large number of aircraft. Some of the navigation tasks, such as flight to the loiter area, loitering, flight to the area of targets with known coordinates and flight along a designated route, are automated. The mission equipment engineers operate the radar and other mission avionics and monitor their health.

The A-50 usually works with Mikoyan MiG-31 *Foxhound* interceptors, though the MiG-31's powerful Phazotron RP-31 *Za**slon***

(Shield) phased-array pulse-Doppler radar enables it to act as a 'mini-AWACS' in its own right. Target data are transmitted to the interceptors and ground C³I centres automatically via data link or by secure voice link. Transmission range to ground C³I centres is 350 km (217 miles) in the metre and decimetre wavebands and 2,000 km (1,242 miles) in the UHF range; SATCOM equipment is used over longer distances.

Pilots are quick to give nicknames to aircraft – affectionate or otherwise. The A-50 was dubbed *shesti**krylyy** sera**fim*** (six-winged seraph, a character from Aleksandr S. Pushkin's poem *The Prophet*), alluding both to the numerous aerodynamic surfaces and the 'eye in the sky' role. Yet the *Mainstay* could easily have earned some disparaging

The mission crew of an early A-50 at their workstations featuring large CRT displays. The radar intercept operators are in winter attire, wearing very old-fashioned leather flying helmets and oxygen masks.

Here, by comparison, the RIOs are also in winter attire but wear modern ZSh-7 'bone dome' helmets.

nickname, and with good reason. For one thing, the mission avionics were rather troublesome at first. As a result, the equipment often had to be switched from automatic to manual mode a dozen times in a mission. Also, the equipment was so bulky that there was no room left for a toilet and a galley (no small thing on a long mission), to say nothing of a rest area.

In 1987-89 two A-50s made occasional visits to three bases of the Soviet Union's Western Group of Forces (WGF) stationed in East Germany – Köthen AB, Falkenberg AB and Damgarten AB. After German reunification in October 1990 the A-50 was used in support of the WGF's pullout from Germany in 1991-94, monitoring the ferry flights of Russian Air Force aircraft across Poland and the Baltic states to their new bases in Russia.

The A-50 has been involved in several armed conflicts – both directly and indi-

rectly. During the First Gulf War (Operation *Desert Storm*) in 1990-91 two *Mainstays* took turns patrolling over the Black Sea, continuously monitoring the operations of Iraqi and Allied forces and keeping a watch for stray US cruise missiles which might be heading towards CIS territory.

Of course, the designers never dreamed – even in their worst nightmares – that the A-50 would see action in 'hot' wars on home ground. In 1993-94, when the trouble in the Russian North Caucasus began, the type was used for monitoring the airspace over the region during anti-terrorist operations. When the First Chechen War (1994-96) broke out, a task force of four A-50s was deployed to Privolzhskiy AB near Astrakhan', operating in concert with Sukhoi Su-27 *Flanker-B* and MiG-31 interceptors. On 21st December 1994, ten days after the outbreak of the war, the Russian PVO regained complete control of the skies over Chechnya after a break of almost three years that had passed since the demise of the Soviet Union. The objective was to prevent the Chechen guerrillas from using aircraft for bringing in supplies and ammunition from abroad – or for kamikaze attacks against Russian targets.

9th May 1995 was the first time when the A-50 participated in the military parade in Moscow during the Victory Day 50th Anniversary celebrations (it was the first V-Day flypast over Moscow in a long time, and this has since become a tradition). However, the First Chechen War was still on at the time, and the government was aware that Chechens might attempt a high-profile terrorist attack on this important public holiday. Therefore, in addition to A-50M '50 Red' which participated in the flypast itself, another *Mainstay* was on station near Moscow, monitoring the airspace over the region.

Quite possibly it was the A-50's involvement in the First Chechen War that tipped the scales in the Russian government's decision to grant high state awards to the aircraft's creators. On 16th January 1996 a group of aviation industry and electronics industry specialists and a number of Russian Air Force specialists were awarded the State Prize for Science and Technology. The laureates included Aleksey K. Konstantinov, Ghennadiy S. Panatov and Sergey A. Atayants (all TANTK Beriyev) who received the prestigious award in recognition of their part in the development of the A-50.

As a point of interest, Major Yuriy V. Lonchakov, who captained an A-50 in 1994-95, went on to become a cosmonaut! On 19th April – 1st May 2001 he flew a mission to the International Space Station aboard the Space Shuttle *Endeavor* as part of the 10th expedition to the ISS.

The Second Chechen War (1999-2001) again involved A-50s monitoring the airspace above the war-torn republic and beyond. As of 2000, 22 A-50s/A-50Ms were in service with the Russian Air Force.

After the reorganisation of the Russian Armed Forces in 2009 involving a change of the order of battle and a switch from air regiments to NATO-style 'aviation bases', the A-50 unit at Ivanovo-Severnyy became the 2457th AvB (AEW&C). In line with the latest trend, the operational A-50s have exchanged their Soviet-era red stars for Russian Air Force tricolour stars, and the aircraft are being progressively placed on the government aircraft register with quasi-civil RF-registrations.

The A-50s have become regular participants in Russian Air Force and combined-arms exercises. For example, on 8th February 2012 two Tupolev Tu-95MS *Bear-H* missile strike aircraft and an A-50 flew a training sortie close to Japan, causing the Japanese Air Self-Defence Force to scramble fighters and investigate. In June 2012 the *Mainstay* participated in a command and

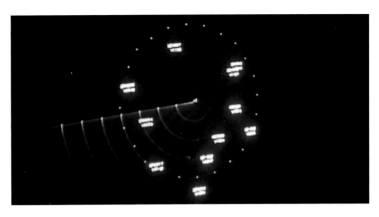

Clockwise from top right: The display of an A-50 radar operator's workstation, with target blips accompanied by relevant information.

Here, the mission crew is in summer camouflaged uniforms and wears only normal headsets.

A-50 *sans suffixe* '33 Red' is refuelled by a TZ-22 at Ivanovo-Severnyy AB. This aircraft has now been upgraded to A-50U standard.

The current version of the unit badge as worn by '33 Red' at the time.

staff exercise which involved some 30 aircraft of the Long-Range Aviation (the Russian Air Force's strategic bomber arm) – specifically, Tu-95MSs and Tu-160s, as well as Il-78M *Midas-B* tankers – and MiG-31 and Su-27 interceptors. The exercise unfolded in the northern regions of Russia, involving redeployment of bombers to forward operating locations. In June 2013 a tactical exercise involving various aircraft types (Mikoyan MiG-29 *Fulcrum-C* fighters, MiG-31 interceptors, Sukhoi Su-24M *Fencer-D* tactical bombers, Antonov An-26 *Curl* and Il-76MD transports, Il'yushin Il-22 *Coot-B* airborne command posts and an A-50) was held in Lipetsk, southern Russia; it was commanded by Maj.-Gen. Aleksandr V. Kharchevskiy, the CO of the Lipetsk-

based 4th Aircrew Training and Hardware Evaluation Centre. In mid-March 2014 A-50 '42 Red'/RF-50610 was deployed to Baranovichi, Belarus, for a joint Russian-Belorussian exercise, supporting the operations of the six participating Russian Air Force Su-27s which flew missions jointly with Belorussian *Fulcrum-Cs*. The most recent example is a joint exercise of the Russian Navy/Baltic Fleet, the Air Force and the Airborne Troops in the Kaliningrad Region exclave in early June 2014, when an A-50 guided Su-27 interceptors, Su-24M and Su-34 *Fullback* tactical bombers to their targets and provided radar coverage. This coincided with the NATO exercises *BaltOps 2014* and *Saber Strike 2014*, so the *Mainstay* kept an eye on these as well.

Opposite page: Accompanied by a quartet of Su-27P interceptors from the Russian PVO's 148th Combat Training & Aircrew Conversion Centre at Savasleyka AB, A-50M '51 Red' flies over the suburbs of Moscow during a rehearsal of the flypast on 9th May 1995 on the occasion of the Victory Day 50th anniversary.

Another public performance. A MiG-31B interceptor coded '05 Blue' breaks formation with an uncoded *Mainstay-A* after a flypast.

Above and left: Seen at Taganrog-Yoozhnyy during modification work at TANTK Beriyev, pristine-looking '30 Red' – the first production A-50 *sans suffixe* – is the sole example to wear a cheatline.

Below: A fine shot of A-50 '30 Red'; the star insignia are still in the old Soviet Air Force style. The aircraft is a 'dogship' used by TANTK Beriyev for testing various improvements, which may account for the non-standard livery.

This page:
A-50M '52 Red' flies over the northern regions of Russia, escorted by a Su-27UB combat trainer carrying R-27R and R-73 missiles.

A-50 '41 Red' passing over Moscow's Red Square during the V-Day parade on 9th May 2010 wears the current Russian Air Force tricolour stars and 'VVS Rossïï' (Russian Air Force) titles on the tail.

Seen here making a flypast at Zhukovskiy during the Russian Air Force Centennial celebrations, A-50 '42 Red' – also in new Russian Air Force insignia – wears the registration RF-50610 in keeping with the current trend. Note the crudely hand-painted 'VVS Rossïï' titles.

Opposite page:
Since the mid-1990s the A-50 has been a regular participant of Russian air parades. Here A-50M '50 Red' makes a flypast in company with upgraded Su-27SM fighters from the Russian Air Force's 4th Combat Training & Aircrew Conversion Centre at Lipetsk-2 AB.

Opposite page, top:
A fine air-to-air of A-50 '41 Red' escorted by Su-27SM '54 Red' and Su-30 '69 Red' from Lipetsk as it flies over northern Moscow on 9th May 2010, heading towards Red Square.

Opposite page, centre and bottom:
The same formation passes over the Kremlin during the 2010 V-Day parade.

This page:
Nice air-to-air pictures of A-50M '50 Red' flying over the Moscow Region during a V-Day parade rehearsal.

This page: A-50 '41 Red'/RF-94268 takes off from runway 12 at Zhukovskiy in August 2012, heading home to Ivanovo after its appearance in the static park at the Russian Air Force Centennial show.

Opposite page: A-50U '47 Red'/RF-92957 makes a flypast at the Russian Air Force Centennial show.

This page:
Overall grey A-50U
'33 Red'/RF-50602 at
Ivanovo-Severnyy in
September 2013.

The same aircraft in the
static park of the
MAKS-2013 airshow
where the upgraded
Mainstay had its public
debut.

A-50U '33 Red'/
RF-50602 departs
Zhukovskiy after the
MAKS-2013 airshow.

Opposite page:
A fine view of A-50U
'33 Red'/RF-50602 from
the refuelling systems
operator's station of an
IL-78M.

The crew of A-50U
'37 Red' pose with the
aircraft during the
redelivery ceremony on
25th March 2014. The
aircraft has been
named 'Sergey
Atayants'.

A-50U '37 Red' flies over the Moscow Channel en route to Red Square during the rehearsal on 7th May 2014.

An atmospheric sunset shot of an A-50U. The *Mainstay* is the guardian of the Russian skies and will continue to be it in the foreseeable future.

The A-50 in Detail

The following brief structural description applies to the production A-50. The fuselage is a semi-monocoque stressed-skin fail-safe structure with frames, longerons and stringers; chemical milling is used on some panels. The riveted fuselage structure is made mainly of D16T duralumin; some parts are made of V93 and V95 aluminium alloys. The greater part of the fuselage is pressurised, with a pressure differential of 0.5 ± 0.02 kg/cm² (7.14 ± 0.28 psi). The cross-section changes from elliptical with the longer axis vertical (up to frame 18) to circular (frames 18-64) to elliptical with the longer axis horizontal (frames 64-95). Maximum fuselage diameter is 4.8 m (15 ft 8⁶³⁄₆₄ in).

Structurally the fuselage is made up of four sections joined by flanges. The forward fuselage (Section F1, frames 1-18) includes the flight crew section and the foremost portion of the mission crew cabin. The former is a double-deck structure with the flight deck above and the navigator's station below; both are accessed from the mission crew cabin via a a pressure door on the starboard side. The flight deck features four optically flat birdproof triplex glass panes at the front; the curved side windows (two of which are sliding direct vision windows doubling as emergency exits) and the eyebrow windows are made of Plexiglas. The navigator's station has a single window on each side (A-50 *sans suffixe*) or just one window to starboard

(A-50M). The glazing (except the windshield panes) features gold plating to protect the crew against the ultra-high-frequency radiation emitted by the radar. An inward-opening dorsal escape hatch (frames 13-14) provides access to the inflatable rescue dinghy in the event of ditching and generally to the upper surface for maintenance purposes. The forward pressure bulkhead mounts the weather radar dish covered by a detachable GRP radome. A chin radome of similar design encloses the ground mapping radar antenna mounted under the pressure floor of the navigator's station; the space between the two radomes is occupied by an ESM antenna under a wraparound GRP fairing. An avionics bay is located ahead of the flight deck (frames 1-3). The nosewheel well is located between frames 11-18. The forward-hinged (outward-opening) entry door is located on the starboard side (frames 15-17). A flight crew escape hatch with a sloping chute and a hydraulically actuated door acting as a slipstream deflector is provided on the port side (frames 9-11).

The centre fuselage (Section F2, frames 18-67) accommodates the mission crew cabin and the mission avionics; the two are separated by a wire mesh screen for protection against UHF radiation. The rear portion has a cutout starting at frame 56 which is closed by the cargo ramp extending to frame 69. The ramp can be opened, allowing the mission crew to bail out in an emergency; it

The flight deck section of an A-50 *sans suffixe*. Note the navigation radar radome and the ESM antenna fairing ahead of it. The rear end of the lateral ECM antenna blister incorporates a wing/air intake inspection light.

The IFR probe and the retractable drogue illumination light associated with it. The weather radar radome is held in place by four prominent locks. Note that the port window of the navigator's station has been blanked off.

The forward fuselage of an A-50U. Most of the windows have gold plating protecting the crew against harmful HF radiation. Note the outlined escape chute and the 'cut here in emergency' stencils.

incorporates a U-shaped tail bumper. Section F2 terminates in a flat rear pressure bulkhead. The wing/fuselage joint is enclosed by an unpressurised fairing, the front half of which (frames 24-29) houses air conditioning system components, the slat drive motor and the rescue dinghy. A large GRP fairing enclosing SATCOM antennas is located ahead of this fairing. The rear half of the wing/fuselage fairing (frames 41-45) houses the flap drive motor, aileron and spoiler controls, and hydraulic equipment. An emergency exit with a window is provided on the starboard side ahead of the wings (frames 23-24) and two more aft of the wings (frames 58-60). One more window is provided on each side between frames 50-51 (just aft of the wing trailing edge). Again, all windows have gold plating.

Two pressurised stowage compartments accessible from outside are located under the floor between frames 18-35 and 51-56. The space between them is occupied by the mainwheel wells separated by the fuselage keel beam. Two elongated fairings of quasi-triangular section are located between frames 26-62, enclosing the main gear fulcrums and actuators; they accommodate the APU, refuelling connectors, DC batteries, liquid oxygen converter, communications and navigation equipment, and some of the mission avionics suite's ancillary systems. The rear portions of the fairings carry large horizontal flat-plate strakes with a straight leading edge and an ogival trailing edge. Two ventral fairings of semi-circular section located side by side enclose the mainwheels.

Two tapered inward-canted pylons of symmetrical airfoil section are mounted aft of the wings, carrying a support structure for the RA-10 rotodome; they incorporate vertical tunnels for the antenna waveguides and

The nose of an A-50M. Note the lack of the port side navigator's station window and the matt off-white sector ahead of the ECM antenna blister, both typical features of the M version.

The centre fuselage, showing the APU air intake and exhaust and the port rear emergency exit. Note the reinforcement plates riveted on for better fatigue resistance.

power cables. The rotodome has a diameter of 10.8 m (35 ft 5⁵⁄₁₆ in) and is 2 m (6 ft 6¾ in) deep. It features a full-width metal support structure of almost rectangular planform incorporating a bearing, a hydraulic drive unit and maintenance hatches; this carries two identical shells of GRP honeycomb construction enclosing the main antenna of the Shmel' radar and the active IFF system.

The unpressurised rear fuselage (Section F3, frames 67-90) carries the vertical tail attached to eight mainframes; it incorporates various aerials and equipment items. The tail section (Section F4, frames 90-95) is an avionics bay. Two ESM antenna arrays covered by GRP fairings are mounted at the rear of this section.

The cantilever shoulder-mounted wings of basically trapezoidal planform are swept back 25° at quarter-chord, with 3° anhedral from roots; incidence 3°, camber –3°, aspect ratio 8.5, taper 1.61. The wings utilise TsAGI high-speed airfoils with a thickness/chord ratio of 13% at root and 10% at tip. They are a stressed-skin structure made of D16T duralumin and built in five pieces: the three-spar centre section integral with the fuselage (the spars are attached to mainframes 29, 34 and 41), three-spar inner wing sections and two-spar outer wing sections with detachable tip fairings. The wing sections are joined by fittings on the upper surface and splice plates on the undersurface. The wing skins are chemically milled with integral stringers and incorporate numerous removable panels for inspection of the integral fuel tanks; the leading and trailing edge portions feature hinged ventral panels for access to con-

The rotodome and its pylons; the latter have leading-edge de-icers. Note the criss-cross lines on the dielectric parts.

trol runs, hydraulic and fuel lines, flap and slat drive shafts and electric cables.

Two engine pylons are attached to each inner wing at ribs 10-11 and 17-18. The inner and outer pylons are respectively 6.35 m (20 ft 10 in) and 10.6 m (34 ft 9²¹⁄₆₄ in) from the fuselage centreline.

The wings are equipped with two-section triple-slotted flaps (one section on each inner and outer wing), five-section leading-edge slats (two inboard and three outboard sections), two-section ailerons, four-section airbrakes on the inner wings and four-section spoilers/lift dumpers on the outer wings. The flaps move on external tracks enclosed by fairings (four on each inboard flap and three on each outboard flap). Flap settings are 15° or 30° for take-off and 43° inboard/41° outboard for landing; the slats are deployed 14° (at 15° flap) or 25°. The ailerons have trim tabs on the outer sections and servo tabs on the inner sections; the travel limits are 28±1° up and 16±1° down. Maximum airbrake and spoiler deflection is 40° and 20° respectively.

The cantilever T-tail of stressed-skin construction is made of D16T duralumin. The vertical tail swept back 39° at quarter-chord consists of a fin and one-piece rudder. The fin is a three-spar structure with 20 ribs; the spars are attached to fuselage mainframes 74, 82 and 86, with five auxiliary fittings in between. A small curved root fillet is attached to the centre and aft fuselage (frames 62-72); it incorporates a large cooling air intake at the root. The rudder is carried on three mounting brackets and an upper support structure, with a travel limit of ±28° 30'; it features a servo tab and a trim tab occupying the entire trailing edge. The horizontal tail swept back 32° at quarter-chord is hinged to the centre spar and consists of two stabilisers and one-piece elevators with a travel limit of 21±1° up and 15±1° down. Stabiliser incidence is adjusted within +2°/–8° by an electric screwjack. Each stabiliser has two spars, 22 ribs and a rounded tip fairing; each elevator is carried on five brackets and one root support, incorporating a geared tab. The fin/stabiliser joint is enclosed by a large area-ruled bullet fairing.

The hydraulically-retractable tricycle landing gear, with free-fall extension in emergency, comprises five units, each with four wheels on a single axle (in pairs on each side of the oleo). All units have oleo-pneumatic shock absorbers. The forward-retracting levered-suspension nose unit has 1,100 x 330 mm (43.3 x 13.0 in) KT-159 wheels and is equipped with a shimmy damper. The inward-retracting main units are located fore and aft of the aircraft's CG and have 1,300 x 480 mm (51.2 x 18.9 in) KT-158 wheels. All wheels have multi-disc brakes. During retraction the mainwheel axles rotate around the oleos by means of mechanical links so that the wheels stow vertically in two semi-circular-section ventral fairings with the axles parallel to the fuselage axis; the axles of the forward pair rotate forward and the axles of the aft pair rotate aft. A safety feature prevents the landing gear from being retracted when the oleos are compressed. The nosewheel well is closed by two pairs of doors. Each main unit has a large curved main door attached to the fuselage keel beam, small double doors in the lateral main gear fairings near the oleos and a small door segment hinged to the oleo itself. All doors open only when the gear is in transit. The steerable nose unit can turn ±50° for taxiing; steering is assisted by differential braking, enabling the aircraft to make a U-turn on a runway 40 m (131 ft) wide. Tyre pressure can be adjusted in flight between 2.5-5 bars (36-73 psi) to suit different types of runways.

The powerplant consists of four Solov'yov (Aviadvigatel') D-30KP Srs 2 turbofans rated at 12,500 kgp (27,560 lbst) for take-off, with a cruise rating of 2,750 kgp (6,060 lbst) at 11,000 m (36,090 ft) and Mach 0.8. The D-30KP is a two-spool turbofan with a three-stage low-pressure (LP) compressor, an 11-stage high-pressure (HP) compressor, a cannular combustion chamber, a two-stage HP turbine, a four-stage LP turbine, a fixed-area jetpipe with a 16-chute core/bypass flow mixer, and a clamshell thrust reverser. Bypass ratio 2.42; overall engine pressure ratio 20, mass flow at take-off 269 kg/sec (593 lb/sec); specific fuel consumption 0.49 kg/kgp·h (lb/lbst·h) at take-off thrust and 0.7 kg/kgp·h in cruise mode. Length overall 5.7 m (18 ft 8¹³⁄₃₂ in), inlet diameter 1.464 m (4 ft 9⁴¹⁄₆₄ in); dry weight 2,650 kg (5,840 lb). Construction is mostly of titanium alloy, with steel used for some HP compressor parts. The LP spool rotates in three bearings: a roller bearing in the air intake assembly, a ball bearing in the division casing and a roller bearing in the rear support frame. The HP spool likewise has three bearings: a roller bearing in the division casing, a ball thrust bearing at the rear of the compressor and a roller bearing ahead of the turbine. The air intake assembly has a fixed spinner and 26 cambered inlet guide vanes (IGVs) de-iced by hot air bled from the 6th or 11th compressor stage; variable IGVs are used on the HP compressor to minimise blade vibration. The division casing is made of magnesium alloy. The combustion chamber has 12 flame tubes, two of which feature igniters. HP turbine blades are cooled by engine bleed air, while LP turbine blades are uncooled. Two ventral accessory gearboxes are provided, one of which has a constant-speed drive for the AC generator and starter. The lubrication system incorporates a fuel/oil heat exchanger and uses VNII NP-50-1-4F synthetic oil or equivalent. The engine is started by an STV-4 air turbine starter (star**tyor** voz**doosh**nyy); time from start to idle is 40-80 seconds, depending on the ambient temperature (operational limits are –60°/+50°C; –76°/+122°F). In-flight starting by windmilling is possible at up to 9,000 m (29,530 ft).

The rear fuselage with the rear ECM blisters and ESM antenna fairings.

Opposite page:
The rear fuselage and tail unit. The A-50M's strap-on flare dispensers are visible here.

The engines are mounted in individual nacelles on forward-swept pylons. Strictly speaking, there are no nacelles as such; each engine has a one-piece annular forward fairing, four hinged cowling panels and a multi-segment rear fairing, all of which are attached directly to the engine casing and can be removed, leaving the engine on the wing.

A Stoopino Machinery Design Bureau TA-6A auxiliary power unit is installed in the rear portion of the port main gear fairing for self-contained engine starting, AC/DC ground power supply and air conditioning. The APU has a dorsal 'elephant's ear' air intake, a one-piece cowling panel and a downward-angled exhaust.

The flight control system has irreversible hydraulic actuators throughout; the actuators are self-contained units, each with its own hydraulic reservoir and electric pump. There is a manual emergency back-up mode with conventional mechanical controls (push-pull rods, cranks and levers). The control runs are duplicated (except rudder control) and routed along opposite sides of the fuselage for greater survivability. Roll control is assisted by the spoilers/lift dumpers on outer wings. An autopilot is fitted.

All fuel is stored in 12 integral tanks in the wing torsion box; two vent surge tanks with pressurisation air scoops under the wingtips are also provided. The fuel tanks are split into four groups, one for each engine; each group has a service tank from which fuel is fed to the engine. Fuel system operation is completely automatic. The A-50 has single-point pressure refuelling; the connectors are located on the starboard main gear fairing between the main gear units. A pneumatically operated telescopic IFR probe is located ahead of the flight deck glazing and connected to the main tanks by a fuel transfer line running along the starboard side of the fuselage. An emergency fuel jettison system is provided. Fuel grades used are Russian T-1 and TS-1 kerosene, Western Jet A-1, DERD.2494 and 2498 (NATO F35 and F43) or equivalent. An inert gas pressurisation system is provided to pressurise the fuel tanks and reduce the hazard of explosion if hit by enemy fire.

Two separate hydraulic systems power the landing gear, flaps, slats, airbrakes, spoilers/lift dumpers and, if required, the entry door, cargo ramp and escape chute door.

Primary 115 V/400 Hz AC power is supplied by engine-driven generators and APU generator. The electric system includes 27 V DC converters; backup power is provided by four DC batteries in the main gear fairings. The AC and DC ground power receptacles are under the front end of the starboard main gear fairing.

Liquid oxygen (LOX) bottles and a LOX converter are installed in one of the main gear fairings to provide breathing oxygen for the crew. The crew sections are pressurised by engine bleed air which is cooled by two heat exchangers located in the forward portion of the wing/fuselage fairing.

The fire suppression system features three groups of fire extinguisher bottles charged with $114V_2$ grade chlorofluorocarbon extinguishing agent for each engine. The first shot is triggered automatically by flame sensors in the engine nacelles; the second and third shots are manually operated. A separate fire extinguisher for the APU bay.

The wing leading edge and engine air intakes are de-iced by engine bleed air. The

The nose landing gear unit.

The main landing gear units and the landing gear fairings with heat exchanger air intakes.

tail unit, windscreens, pitot heads and static ports have electric de-icing.

The A-50 is fully equipped for all-weather day/night operation. Navigation and piloting equipment includes an SAU-1T-2BT automatic flight control system (*sistema avtomatichheskovo oopravleniya*), a DISS-013-S2 or DISS-013-S2M Doppler speed/drift sensor (*doplerovskiy izmeritel' skorosti i snosa*), an RLS-N weather radar (*rahdiolokatsionnaya stahntsiya* – radar), an RLS-P *Koopol* (Dome – or parachute canopy) ground mapping radar, a central digital navigation computer, a TKS-P precision compass system (*tochnaya koorsovaya sistema*), a duplex I-P-76 inertial navigation system and an RSBN-7S *Vstrecha* (Rendezvous) short-range radio navigation system. The aircraft is equipped with an instrument landing system permitting ICAO Cat II automatic approach, with Koors-MP-2 and Koors-MP-70 automatic approach systems, RV-5 and RV-5M radio altimeters (*rahdiovysotomer*) linked to a Vektor ground proximity warning system, an ARK-15M automatic direction finder (*avtomatichheskiy rahdiokompas* – ADF), SD-75 and SDK-67 distance measuring equipment (*samolyotnyy dahl'nomer* – DME).

Communications equipment includes R-855UM, R-855A1 and R-861 UHF radios with dorsal and ventral blade aerials on the forward fuselage, main and backup *Mikron* (Micron) and *Yadro* (Core) VHF radios with antennas buried in the fin bullet fairing, and an R-851 emergency radio beacon. SPU-8 and SPU-15 intercoms (*samolyotnoye peregovornoye oostroystvo*) are provided. An RI-65 automatic voice annunciator (*rechevoy informahtor*) warns the crew of critical failures (fire etc.) and dangerous flight modes.

The A-50 is equipped with a Shmel' early warning and control suite. This comprises a pulse-Doppler search radar with a 360° field of view, a digital data processing system, a radar data presentation system with operators' consoles, an IFF interrogation system, a data link system for transmitting target data to 'friendly' fighters or C³I centres, encoding/decoding equipment and a data recording system.

The aircraft features an SRO-1P *Parol'* (Password, aka *izdeliye* 62-01) IFF transponder with blade aerials are located ahead of the flight deck glazing and under fuselage section F4, as well as SOM-64, SO-70 and SO-72M air traffic control (ATC) transponders. ECM and ESM equipment comprises an S-3M Sirena-2 radar homing and warning system, an active ECM system with four (or six, on the A-50M) emitter antennas in teardrop fairings on the fuselage sides to give 360° coverage, ESM antennas in the fuselage nose and tailcone. Infra-red countermeasures are provided by flare dispensers built into the rear fuselage underside to fire 50-mm (1⁶³⁄₆₄-in) PPI-50 magnesium flares; the A-50M additionally has podded 96-round flare dispensers scabbed onto the rear fuselage sides.

Two of the radar intercept operators' workstations of an A-50 *sans suffixe*.

■ A-50 SPECIFICATIONS

Length overall	
(less IFR probe)	46.59 m (152 ft 10¼ in)
Wing span	50.5 m (165 ft 8in)
Height on ground	14.76 m (48 ft 5 in)
Wing area	300.0 m² (3,229.2 sq ft)
Stabiliser span	17.4 m (57 ft 1³⁄₆₄ in)
Landing gear track	8.16 m (26 ft 9¼ in)
Maximum take-off weight	190,000 kg (418,875 lb)
Maximum landing weight	165,000 kg (363,760 lb)
Internal fuel load	64,820 kg (142,900 lb)
Cruising speed	800 km/h (496 mph)
Service ceiling	12,000 m (39,370 ft)
Effective range	7,500 km (4,660 miles)
On-station loiter altitude	8,000-10,000 m
	(26,250-32,810 ft)
On-station loiter speed	600 km/h (372 mph)
On-station loiter time:	
1,000 km (621 miles) from base	4 hours
2,000 km (1,242 miles) from base	1.4 hours
Range on internal fuel	7,000 km (4,350 miles)
Endurance	7 hours
Overland coverage against	
fighter-type targets	230 km (142 miles)
Coverage against large ships	400 km (248 miles)
Number of targets	
tracked at a time	Up to 50
guided at a time	Up to 10
Data link range:	
VHF/UHF comm	350 km (217 miles)s
HF comms	2,000 km (1,242 miles)
SATCOM	more than 2,000 km

■ A-50 FAMILY FLEET LIST

C/n	F/n	Type	Code/serial/registration	Notes
073409243	0701	A-50	SovAF '10 Red'	First prototype, converted from Il-76 CCCP-86641; f/f 19-12-1978. Stored Taganrog-Yoozhnyy
073410311	0808	A-50	SovAF '15 Red'	Second prototype, converted from Il-76. Stored Taganrog-Tsentrahl'nyy AB
0013430875	2209A	A-50	SovAF '20 Red'	Third prototype, converted from Il-76M
0023436059	2705	A-50	SovAF/RusAF '30 Red'	Active; non-standard c/s with blue/white cheatline
0033443258	3205	A-50	SovAF/RusAF '46 Red'	First aircraft thus coded. Stored Staraya Roossa
0033447379	3505	A-50	SovAF/RusAF '38 Red'	Stored
0043449460	3705	A-50	SovAF/RusAF '34 Red'	Active
0043451498	3805	A-50	SovAF/RusAF '46 Red'	Second aircraft thus coded. TANTK development aircraft. Scrapped Taganrog-Yoozhnyy 1993
0043452537	3905	A-50	SovAF/RusAF '39 Red'	Active
0043453577	4005	A-50	SovAF/RusAF '47 Red'	Converted to, see next line
		A-50U	'47 Red'/RF-92957	First 'production' upgrade
0043454618	4105	A-50	SovAF/RusAF '33 Red'	Converted to, see next line
		A-50U	'33 Red'/RF-50602	Second 'production' upgrade; named 'Vladimir Ivanov', overall dark grey c/s
0063458738	4405	A-50	SovAF/RusAF '48 Red'	Active
0053459777	4505	A-50	SovAF/RusAF '31 Red'	Active
0063466979	5005	A-50	SovAF/RusAF '32 Red'	Active
0063469057	5205	A-50	SovAF/RusAF '49 Red'	Active
0063473178	5505	A-50	SovAF/RusAF '35 Red'	Active
0073475260	5705	A-50	SovAF/RusAF '36 Red'	Active
0073476298	5805	A-50	SovAF/RusAF '37 Red'	Converted to, see next line
		A-50U	'37 Red'/RF-93966	Prototype, named 'Sergey Atayants'
0073479377	6005	A-50	SovAF/RusAF '43 Red'	
			'43 Red'/RF-50608	Active
0083481457	6205	A-50	SovAF/RusAF '40 Red'	Active
0083483499	6305	A-50	SovAF/RusAF '41 Red'	
			'41 Red'/RF-94268	Active
0093484538	6405	A-50	SovAF/RusAF '42 Red'	
			'42 Red'/RF-50610	Active
0093486579	6505	A-50M	SovAF/RusAF '44 Red'	Prototype. Converted to, see next line
		A-50I	no registration	Became, see next line
			RA-78740	Became, see next line
			4X-AGI	Became, see next line
			RA-78740	Converted to, see next line
		KJ-2000	762 Black	Prototype, CFTE. Stored Xian-Yanliang
1003488634	6609	A-50M	SovAF/RusAF '51 Red'	
			'51 Red'/RF-50606	Active
1013491739	6905	A-50M	SovAF/RusAF '52 Red'	Stored Taganrog-Yoozhnyy 2011/on overhaul
0093493818	7105	A-50M	SovAF/RusAF '45 Red'	Active
1003496899	7305	A-50M	SovAF/RusAF '50 Red'	
			'50 Red'/RF-50601	Active
0093497940	7405	A-50M	SovAF/RusAF '53 Red'	Stored. Possibly not completed/delivered
2053421727	9402	A-50EI	KW-3551	50 Sqn
2053421730	9403	A-50EI	KW-3552	50 Sqn
2053421736	9404	A-50EI	KW-3553	50 Sqn
1063421737	9405	(Il-76TD)	no registration	To be completed as an A-50EI?
1073422753	9409	(Il-76TD)	no registration	To be completed as an A-50EI?
0063465965	5002	'Aircraft 976'	CCCP-76452	Stored Zhukovskiy
0063466995	5009	'Aircraft 976'	CCCP-76453	Became, see next line
			RA-76453	Active
0073469074	5209	'Aircraft 976'	CCCP-76454	Converted to, see next line
		Il-76LL	76454	LII
0063471125	5402	'Aircraft 976'	CCCP-76455	Became, see next line
			76455	Stored Zhukovskiy
0073474208	5602	'Aircraft 976'	CCCP-76456	Converted to, see next line
		Il-76LL	76456	Sold to China. Became, see next line
			760 Black	CFTE
0013430888	2302	KJ-2000	'YH2000'	Ground test article, converted from Il-76TD RA-76458
0043449471	3708	KJ-2000	no registration	Ground test article, converted from Il-76MD (UR-)76579
1063418587	9007	KJ-2000	B-4042	Converted Il-76MD 'Falsie'. Became, see next line
			30073 Red	26th Special Mission Air Division/76th Regiment
1053419656	9204	KJ-2000	B-4040	Converted Il-76MD 'Falsie'. Became, see next line
			30071 Red	26th Special Mission Air Division/76th Regiment
1053420663	9206	KJ-2000	B-4041	Converted Il-76MD 'Falsie'. Became, see next line
			30072 Red	26th Special Mission Air Division/76th Regiment
1063420671	9208	KJ-2000	B-4043	Converted Il-76MD 'Falsie'. Became, see next line
			30074 Red	26th Special Mission Air Division/76th Regiment
?	?	Baghdad-1	no serial (IrAF)	Converted Il-76MD 'Falsie' YI-AN… Became, see next line
		?	IRIAF 5-8205	Chipped grey/white c/s with thin black cheatline, '7' on tail to denote Tactical Air Base 7, serial in European characters, no titles. Wfu Tehran-Mehrabad by 4-2009
0083484542	6406	Adnan-1	no serial (IrAF)	Converted Il-76MD 'Falsie' YI-ANL. Became, see next line
			IRIAF 5-8208	Grey/white c/s with thin black cheatline, no titles, serial in Farsi, no titles. Crashed near Varamin 22-9-2009
?	?	Adnan-2	no serial (IrAF)	Converted Il-76MD 'Falsie'. Destroyed 1990

The Modeller's Corner

1:72nd scale

While special mission aircraft in general, and AWACS aircraft in particular, do have their 'own little legion of fans', they are nowhere near as popular with modellers as fighters, bombers and other combat aircraft. Therefore, model kits covering the subject are unsurprisingly few. So far, four kits of the A-50 are known, and three of them are to 1:72nd scale.

The first of these was released in the early 1990s by the Ukrainian manufacturer **YuMTK**, a small private enterprise based in the town of Vasil'kov (Kiev Region). Little is known about it except that it was a vacuform kit and it was based on the manufacturer's Il-76 kit – one of the first-ever kits of the *Candid*. YuMTK have long since gone out of business, and their A-50 kit is no longer available.

The second kit is likewise a vacuform produced by the Welsh company **Sanger** (aka **Sanger-Contrail**) based in Carmarthen, Carmarthenshire. Unsurprisingly, the evolution of the model echoes the evolution of the real thing; the A-50 kit (Ref. No.CON740) is based on Sanger's Il-76 kit (Ref. No.CON739), with the addition of some *Mainstay*-specific parts – the rotodome and its pylons, the vertical tail featuring the fin root air intake, and the SATNAV antenna fairing; the rest of the parts are the same. The large and drab-looking cardboard box contains white polystyrene sheet of 1 mm, 1.25 mm, 1.5 mm and 2 mm thickness with a total of 107 parts (the fuselage comes in two halves, with no breakdown into smaller sections, and each of the 20 wheels is in two halves). There are two transparencies for the flight deck glazing and 20 parts cast in white metal, including the landing gear struts, the engine air intake assemblies (with the first stage of the LP compressors), the flight crew seats and control columns. The very basic decal sheet features six red stars of the same size (although the ones for the fin should be larger), three alternative serials for A-50s *sans suffixe* '40 Red', '42 Red' and '43 Red' and, for reasons unknown, the CCCP nationality prefix.

Quite apart from the difficulties inherent in building a vacuform model this big, the Sanger kit is rather inaccurate – the main landing gear fairings are taken straight from the Il-76, the distinctive horizontal strakes on the said fairings are missing (interestingly, this is an omission common to *all* kits of the A-50!), the shape of the bullet fairing at the top of the fin is incorrect etc. Also, the

quality of the white metal castings is rather poor, and some modellers chose to use replacement items.

The third kit – the best so far – is by another Ukrainian manufacturer, **Amodel**, which has made a name for itself by catering for modellers who want something outside the mainstream. As a rule, Amodel offers injection moulded polystyrene kits, using the 'short run' technology. However, in the case of the 1:72nd scale heavy aircraft series (aptly dubbed 'Amonsters' by the modellers because of the finished models' impressive size) polystyrene would not be strong enough, so the principal airframe components are made of glassfibre reinforced plastic (GRP) – to be precise, glassfibre reinforced epoxy resin (commonly referred to simply as 'fibreglass resin'). This should give a high-quality surface finish while making for a sufficiently rigid structure, but requires Superglue to join the parts.

Again, the A-50 kit (Ref. No.72019) released in the early 2000s is derived from Amodel's Il-76 kit (Ref. No.72012) – to be precise, the Il-76MD. The huge box contains no fewer than 435 parts, and the finished model is an impressive 660 mm (25$^{63}\!/_{64}$ in) long, with a wing span of 704 mm (27$^{23}\!/_{32}$ in). The bilingual (English/Russian) assembly instructions are quite detailed and give Humbrol enamel numbers as a painting guide. Nevertheless, this is definitely a project for the seasoned modeller, and the manufacturer honestly advises of this on the box.

In the original Il-76 kit the fuselage breakdown is almost exactly as on the actual aircraft: there are two large prefabricated parts made of light grey GRP – the forward

The box top of Sanger-Contrail's A-50 kit.

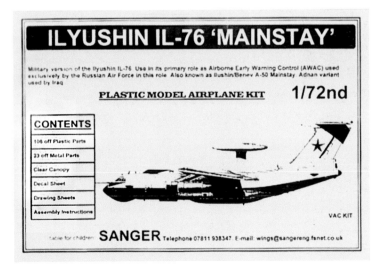

The Sanger-Contrail A-50 built by a Russian modeller with the Internet alias Serg62 around 1998. The stock engine air intakes, landing gear struts and wheels were replaced with scratchbuilt items or parts from the spares box; so were the decals (which accounts for the inappropriate tactical code). The glazing was fashioned from Plexiglas. The model was painted with automotive enamels and nitrocellulose paints.v

The box top of
Amodel's 'Amonster'
A-50 kit.

fuselage (section F1) and the centre/rear fuselage (sections F2/F3 together), which is manufactured integrally with the wing centre section and the fin – and the tail section (the gunner's station, section F4), which is assembled from injection moulded parts. However, since the fuselage of the A-50 is considerably different (there are no cargo doors and no port side entry door, the lateral main gear fairings have a different shape, section F4 is a windowless avionics bay etc.), Amodel wisely chose to design the fuselage for the A-50 kit anew. The wings come as one-piece GRP parts with two alignment pegs on the 'root ribs' fitting into holes on the centre section 'ribs', so care must be taken during assembly to ensure the correct 3° anhedral; the stabilisers and the fin top bullet fairing are manufactured as a single GRP subassembly. The rotodome itself is prefabricated from GRP, while its pylons (like almost all the remaining parts) are moulded in white polystyrene. All major components feature finely engraved panel lines.

Speaking of injection moulded parts, the box contains six Baggies chock full of sprues with small items! The clear sprue features mainly the flight deck roof with its numerous windows (which obviously require masking, once the item has been glued, filled and sanded before priming and painting). A shame that not much of the interior will be visible once the thing has been painted, as the flight deck is extremely detailed – only the seat belts and throttles are missing. There are also a few photo-etched parts such as aerials and air vents. Somewhat surprisingly, the decal sheet is the same for the A-50 and the Il'yushin/Beriyev A-60 airborne laser laboratory (Ref. No.72025); thus, in addition to two large Soviet Air Force stars for the A-50's tail, four smaller stars for the wings, the tactical codes '17 Red' (dubious) and '42 Red' (correct), and the round squadron badge of the AWACS unit based at Ivanovo-Severnyy AB (two of these are included, although the badge is applied only

the starboard side only) it includes irrelevant Aeroflot titles/logos and the registration CCCP-86879 for the A-60!

Like the Il-76 kit, the A-50 kit has a few 'action' features. The ailerons, rudder and elevators are separate injection moulded items and can be set at an angle; the stabilisers are attached to the fin by a short axle at the would-be rear spar which allows sta-

Some of the GRP
subassemblies of the
Amodel kit – the
fuselage and the
rotodome.

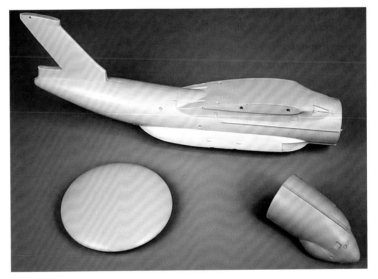

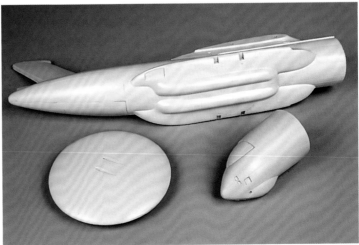

biliser incidence to be varied. (However, the flaps and leading-edge slats are manufactured integrally – that is, in the retracted position, whereas having the stabilisers at full –8° take-off/landing incidence would look odd without the high-lift devices deployed!) The clamshell thrust reverser doors of all four engines are separate items and can be assembled in the open position; however, here the instruction contains an error, and if you do it 'by the book' it is impossible to have the reversers fully deployed.

For all its merits, the Amodel A-50 does have its share of bugs. The most glaring error is the omission of the sole entry door on the starboard side – the designers of the model must have got carried away or have forgotten something; thus, the modeller has to reinstate that door. Another serious gaffe is that while the APU air intake (which has the right size but the wrong shape, being more similar to that of the KJ-2000) is correctly positioned on the port main gear fairing, the recess for the injection moulded APU jetpipe is on the underside of the *starboard* main gear fairing! The jetpipe must be relocated or built from scratch, and the offend-

ing recess must be filled and sanded flush. There is a couple of unwanted windows amidships (ergo, more filling and sanding). Also, as mentioned earlier, the strakes on the main gear fairings are missing; they have to be fabricated from plastic card and glued into place, using pins. The engine air intakes are another area where there's room for improvement: the intake lips are too sharp and the compressor faces are rather basic, lacking the D-30KP's prominent inlet guide vanes; photo-etched parts would work wonders here.

A few criticisms have to be directed at the manufacturing standards; the prefabricated fuselage sections are glued together from several pieces; the joints between these are rough, requiring sanding – and the resin is very hard. Also, some modellers who have built the A-50 (and the Il-76, for that matter) say the surface finish of the GRP components leaves something to be desired, especially the panel lines on the forward fuselage. One tricky area is the landing gear – each strut consists of 20 (!) parts, and with 20 wheels on five struts it is quite tough to assemble so that the finished model sits with all wheels properly touching the ground.

Opposite and above: Amodel's modified A-50 built by Mikhail Bliznyuk as an A-50M. The model took 11 months to complete. The author took pains to rectify the kit's bugs: the missing horizontal strakes are scratchbuilt, as are the engine compressor assemblies (the stock short-run items were substandard). The missing entry door was rescribed, the APU exhaust was relocated to its proper position on the port side, using a piece of metal tube from a telescopic antenna. Self-adhesive metal foil was used for the de-icers, as well as for correcting the panel lines on the fuselage and reproducing small panels. Scratchbuilt flare dispensers were added. The model has been electrified to feature exterior and interior lighting using LEDs; power is supplied through the base of the diorama, the nosewheels incorporating electric contacts. Acrylic paints were used, with Tamiya enamels for highlighting; the star insignia and tactical code were sprayed on, using masking tape and the unit badge is a homemade decal (the stock decal sheet has codes for an A-50 *sans suffixe* and a different version of the badge). The gold plating on the glazing was simulated, using appropriately coloured gift wrap ribbon cut to shape.

1:44th scale

Here the offer is limited to a single kit. In 2002 the well-known Chinese manufacturer **Trumpeter**, which uses the traditional (high-pressure) injection moulding technique, hit the market with three closely related kits at once – the Il-76MD, Il-78 *sans suffixe* and A-50. Interestingly, the Il-76MD kit has been reboxed in Russia under the Modelist brand (Ref. No.214479) but not the other two kits.

The A-50 kit (Ref. No.03903) differs from the baseline Il-76MD kit (Ref. No.03901) in that sprue G (comprising the three-segment cargo doors, the halves of the tail gunner's station and the cannon barbette) is omitted and substituted with sprue F. This increased the number of parts from 92 to 104; there are six sprues moulded in light grey plastic (which is quite hard) and one small clear sprue. All major parts have engraved panel lines. The finished model is quite large, with a length of 330 mm (almost exactly 13 in) and a wing span of 350 mm ($13^{25}\!/_{32}$ in); apparently the length is less IFR probe, as all three kits have the same dimensions stated on the box. An eight-page fold-out instruction sheet is included, as are decals for a single Soviet Air Force aircraft ('50 Red'); Gunze Sangyo/Mr. Color enamel numbers are used as a painting guide.

The fuselage is in two halves comprising sections F1/F2/F3 and the vertical tail (complete with the fin top fairing), while the tail section (section F4) and the fin fillet are separate parts which are the same on the Il-76MD/Il-78 but different on the A-50. The centre fuselage underside and the cargo ramp are moulded separately (parts E1 and B2; the ramp is no doubt included for the sake of mould commonality). The former part features integrally moulded mainwheel wells, the nosewheel well (part A3) and the

wheel well doors are separate items; this gives you the option of assembling the model with the landing gear extended, retracted or in transit. (It must be noted that the two larger mainwheel well doors on each side are moulded in one piece; so are all four nose-wheel well doors, requiring some cutting, should you wish to have them open.)

The wings are in upper/lower halves, as are the stabilisers. The wing leading edges (that is, the LE slats) come as separate parts; this may tempt you to 'doctor' them a little and show the slats in the deployed position, but that would also require the flaps to be deployed, and reproducing the Il-76's extended double-slotted flaps is quite a task. Each engine nacelle is also in two halves (to be precise, the cowling sections moulded integrally with the pylons, with the annular front and rear sections as separate parts).

The abovementioned sprue F features the upper and lower halves of the rotodome, the pylons for the latter, the two halves of the fuselage tail section, an opaque 'jaw' replacing the one-piece clear moulding for the navigator's station glazing (part H4), the dorsal SATCOM antenna fairing, the lateral ECM blisters, the IFR probe – and two cylindrical wingtip pods replacing the regular wingtips, as an extra!

The 'gooda news' is that assembly is straightforward, the parts are crisply moulded, with no flash, and go together well (though some kit reviewers have contested this, complaining about warped and poorly fitting parts). The fuselage mouldings are identical to those of the Il-76MD, except for the tail section; this, together with the optional wingtip pods and navigator's station glazing (yes, a full set of Il-76MD transparencies is included!), allows you to build the 'aircraft 976'. However, this would

The box top of Trumpeter's A-50 kit.

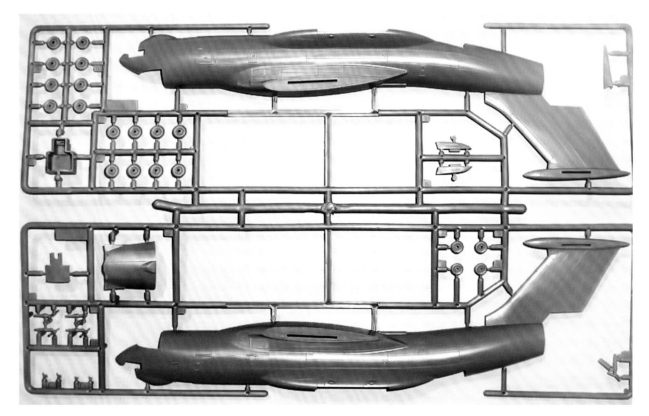

require reinstating the correct gunner's station, scratchbuilding the rear dielectric fairing and the various aerials unique to this version and, of course, using proper decals (a decal sheet for 'aircraft 976' is available as an aftermarket item).

And now, the 'bada news'! Since the fuselage halves have been taken as-is from the Il-76MD kit, the shape of the main gear fairings is wrong and the air intakes in the front ends of these fairings are missing; the telltale horizontal strakes on the rear ends are also missing and have to be fashioned from plastic card. Not only is there an unnecessary port side entry door from the Il-76 but the flight deck escape hatch, which is located ahead of it, is misguidedly repeated on the starboard side of the nose! There is not even a hint of the flight deck interior. The abovementioned 'jaw' is a poor fit, with untidy gaps all around, and the navigator's station windows (of which there should be one or two, after all) are not reproduced if you install this part as-is. On the other hand, the instructions suggest you use the *rear* glazing, which is replaced by a dielectric panel on the real A-50; this transparency (or a scratchbuilt replacement) should be filed and sanded to a more rounded cross-section before gluing and painting to reproduce the shape of the real thing. The engine air intakes are decidedly too small in diameter and require some reaming out at the very least – or, better still, replacement with aftermarket items (see below). The diameter of the rotodome is likewise a bit too small; also, the rotodome pylons have alignment pins at the roots but there are no corresponding holes in the top of the fuselage, and the instruction does not tell you where exactly to drill these holes! While the IFR probe is

Some of the sprues of the Trumpeter kit. Note the fuselage breakdown with interchangeable tail sections for related kits and the wing leading edges moulded as separate parts; sprue F with the *Mainstay*-specific parts features optional parts allowing you to build the 'aircraft 976'.

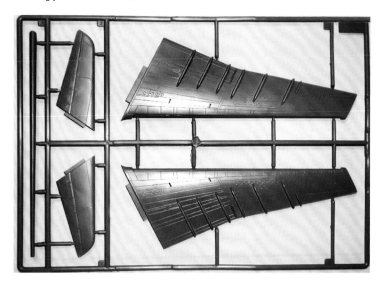

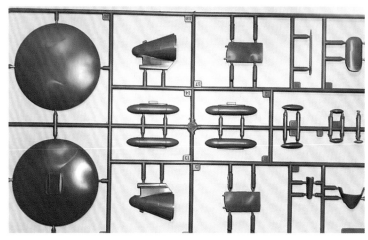

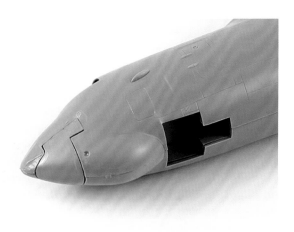

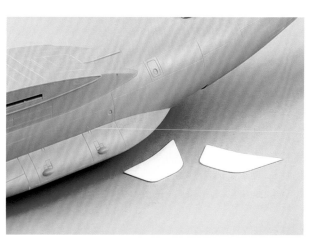

Opposite page:

Top left: The forward fuselage of Trumpeter's A-50; the opaque 'jaw' replacing the navigator's station transparency of the IL-76/IL-78 is a rather poor fit.

Top right: A glaring error common to all A-50 kits is the omission of the horizontal strakes; this is how they have to be manufactured from plastic card.

Centre and bottom: The Trumpeter A-50 built 'out of the box' by Lukasz Kedzierski. The code would suggest an A-50M.

This page:

The Trumpeter A-50 built by Artyom Kamburian. The diameter of the air intakes has been corrected and the heat exchanger intakes have been drilled out; scratchbuilt strakes, ECM blisters, flare dispensers and fuel line conduit have been added.

included, the fuel line conduit for it on the starboard side is not and needs to be added as a scratchbuilt item. The front and rear lateral ECM blisters are of the wrong shape and size; the best thing to do is throw them out and manufacture replacement items. The port midship ECM blister (typical of the A-50M) is included but, oddly enough, not the starboard one; also, the box art and tactical code on the decal sheet show an A-50M, but the strap-on flare dispensers characteristic of this version are not included. The painting instructions are incorrect at times – for example, the interiors of the wheel wells should be beige, not light blue (though they assume a nondescript colour in service due

to dirt deposits). Finally, the stock decal sheet is absolutely no good – all six stars are of the same size, the tactical code has the wrong font, and the pairs of small square dielectric panels on the sides of the nose are ochre – which is correct for the A-50 *sans suffixe* but not for the A-50M, where they should be dark grey.

This page and opposite: The Trumpeter A-50M built by Mike Grant. The diameter of the air intakes has been corrected by reaming out; for want of adequate substitute engine fan parts the air intakes have been blanked off. Unfortunately the incorrect ECM blisters have been used as-is. Scratchbuilt strakes, flare dispensers (looking more like the APP-50 model used on the IL-76MD) and fuel line conduit have been added (the latter is a bit too long) The model is painted with Tamiya paints; the stock decals were substituted with homemade ones (however, '33 Red' is an A-50 *sans suffixe!*).

1:165th scale

Yes, 1:165th! An obscure company from Hong Kong (the manufacturer's name is not indicated on the box) has released a kit to this decidedly non-standard scale. Unusually, the model represents not the A-50 but its Chinese 'cousin', the KJ-2000. The writing on the box top (which is entirely in Chinese) suggests this is a 'snap-tite' model and is number 2 in some series of models.

The kit includes a very limited number of parts moulded in a light bluish grey plastic to replicate the colour scheme of the real thing, obviating the need for painting, and a single transparency for the flight deck glazing; the fixed 'unrotodome' and its pylons come as a one-piece part. The assembled model is approximately 127 mm (5 in) long. The airframe has engraved panel lines, including the plethora of maintenance hatches on the wings, but these are so deep that they look

like 'a full-size trench for a bedbug', to use a phrase coined by a Russian modeller caustically commenting on a different kit. There is no landing gear, but a two-piece stand is included. On the whole, this Chinese 'mongrel' looks more like a toy than a true kit.

Above: The box top of the unidentifiable KJ-2000 kit.

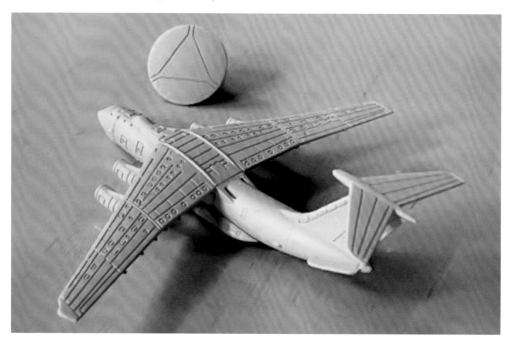

Right and below: The partly assembled 1:165th scale model of the KJ-2000 – crude, to say the least.

Opposite, top and centre: Two sets of resin parts for Trumpeter's A-50 by Bra.Z Models comprising the engine air intakes and the thrust reversers (closed in one set and open in the other set).

Opposite, bottom: The photo-etched parts set for Trumpeter's A-50 by Extra Tech.

AFTERMARKET ITEMS

So far, apparently there are no aftermarket parts for the 1:72nd scale Il-76, A-50 and A-60 kits. This is probably because the kits are expensive (not to mention the huge size of the completed model and the resulting display space problems), hence demand is low and does not justify production of aftermarket items.

The modellers wising to improve the accuracy of their 1:144th scale Il-76MD, Il-78 or A-50 are clearly better off in this respect. Firstly, the Italian company **Bra.Z Models** specialising in limited edition resin kits of aircraft and conversion kits for models by other manufacturers offers three sets of polyester resin parts for the Trumpeter kits. Set 1 (Ref. No.B4KI7S) consists of four engine air intakes of the correct diameter (with integrally cast compressor faces) and four engine nacelle tail sections with the thrust reversers in the normal (closed) position. Set 2 (Ref. No.B4KI7A) consists of 16 parts – the four air intakes, four engine nacelle tail sections with the jetpipes exposed, and eight thrust reverser doors which can be glued in the deployed position (the arms on which they move have to be fashioned from plastic card). Set 3 (Ref. No.B4KWI7) consists of 20 wheels to replace the stock items in the kit.

Secondly, in 2006 the Czech company **Extra Tech** released a set of photo-etched parts (Ref. No.EX 14410) comprising 82 items. These include the engine compressor blades, wheel rims and more – even the boarding ladder.

Thirdly, a Chinese company called **Eleven Model** (*sic*) has released a kit (Ref. No.K005) that allows you to convert Trumpeter's Il-76 into a fairly accurate model of the KJ-2000 (the box top features a specific mention of the Il-76 kit's product code, 04001). The kit includes resin parts (the 'unrotodome' and its pylons, the rear fuselage strakes, the dorsal SATCOM antenna fairing and the wingtip ECM fairings) and a small photo-etched fret for the numerous blade aerials. (Incidentally, the 'serving suggestion' on the box top shows that the lower ends of the aerials are to be bent at right angles for gluing to the fuselage, which looks rather untidy, so the modeller might consider making slits in the fuselage instead.) The decal sheet features PLAAF 'stars and bars' insignia, the Chinese flag and the registration B-4040, allowing you to portray one of the KJ-2000s during the initial service period before it gained full military markings as 30071 Red.

Finally, a decal sheet for Trumpeter's Il-76 is available that lets you complete Trumpeter's A-50 as 'aircraft 976' RA-76455, using the alternative parts in the kit (although, as mentioned earlier, some modifications are still required to the rear extremity of the fuselage to produce a realistic model of the *Mainstay-C*).

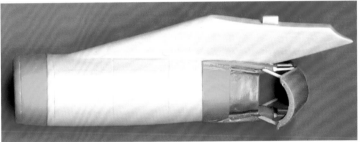

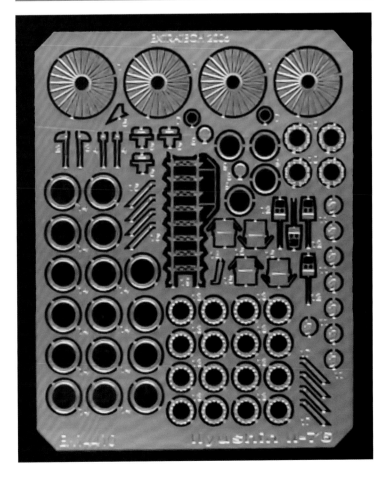

Opposite page:
Overall view of the KJ-2000 converted from Trumpeter's IL-76, using the Eleven Model kit.

This page:
The box top of the Eleven Model KJ-2000 conversion kit.

The forward fuselage of finished model. The aerials and the SATCOM antenna fairing have intentionally been left unpainted here. Perhaps the modeller might consider making slits in the fuselage to fit the aerials more tidily?

The rear fuselage of the converted Trumpeter IL-76 with the ventral fins and the decals in place.

TOYS'R'US?

Below: The 1:100th scale KJ-2000 by Dongguan Aoqi.

Given the dearth of proper A-50 kits, we might as well mention that there are several ready-made scale models of the *Mainstay* and *Mainring* on the market. Thus, the Chinese manufacturer **Dongguan Aoqi High-Quality Model & Toy Co., Ltd.** has released

Above: The 1:200th scale A-50M by Amercom.

Below: The 1:400th scale 'aircraft 976' by Witty Wings in a box improperly marked 'IL-76MD-90A'.

a decent desktop model of the KJ-2000 to 1:100th scale, complete with display stand; the model is in full military markings but with no PLAAF serial. The die-cast company **Gaincorp** has released a 1:130th scale model of A-50M '51 Red' in its World Aircraft Collection series (Ref. No.A50A); the model is 355 mm (14 in) long, with a wing span of 387 mm (15¼ in), and again includes a display stand. **Amercom S.A.**, another die-cast company whose product range includes cars, armoured vehicles and aircraft (none of which are noted for being particularly accurate), offers a model of the same A-50M '51 Red' to 1:200th scale (Ref. No.LB-12) which comes within a partwork series (with a magazine). The model is made of plastic, not metal, and features a display stand.

A die-cast model of 'aircraft 976' (CCCP-76455) to 1:400th scale was manufactured under the **Witty Wings** brand (Ref. No.WTW4176015); oddly, the box is labelled 'Il-76MD-90A' (in Russian!). Finally, a limited-edition die-cast model of another 'aircraft 976', RA-76453, to 1:500th scale by **Inflight 500** (Ref. No.A015-IF5176001) was released in September 2006 with 744 pieces produced. The model is 920 mm (3⅝ in) long, with a wing span of 100 mm (3¹⁵⁄₁₆ in); unfortunately the manufacturer has forgotten an important feature of 'aircraft 976' – the wingtip pods.

Above: The 1:400th scale 'aircraft 976' 76455 by Witty Wings; note that the CCCP- prefix has been removed on the fin but retained on the wings – just like on the actual aircraft!

Below: The 1:500th scale 'aircraft 976' by Inflight 500 – unfortunately without wingtip pods.

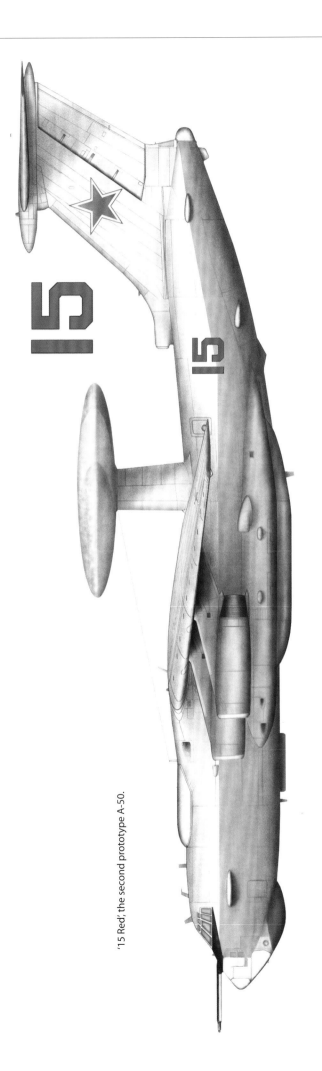

'15 Red', the second prototype A-50.

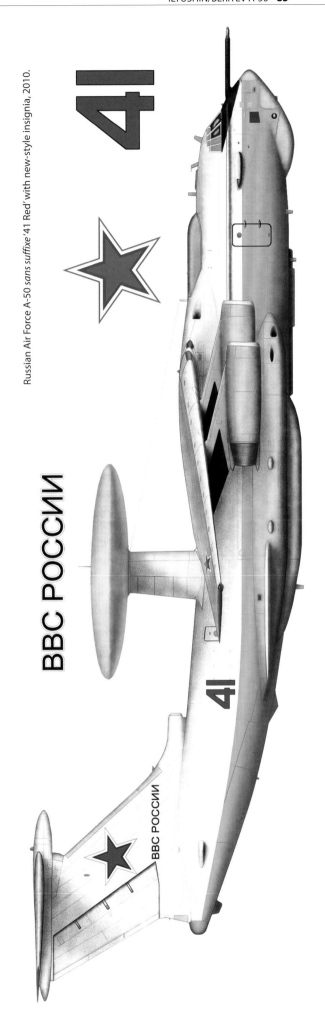

Russian Air Force A-50 *sans suffixe* '41 Red' with new-style insignia, 2010.

ВВС РОССИИ

ВВС РОССИИ

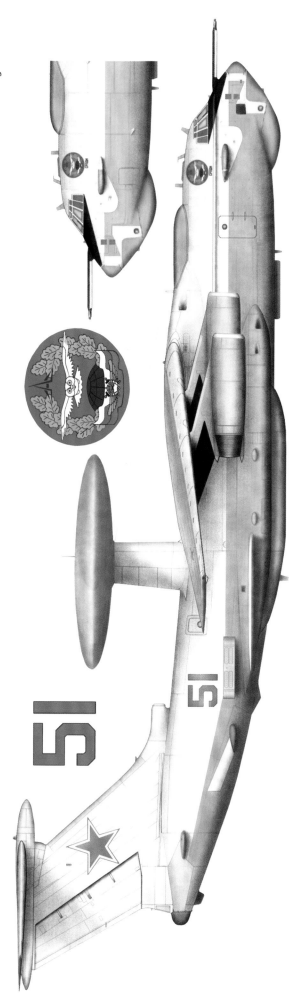

A-50M '51 Red' with the old version of the 2457th AEW&C Unit badge.

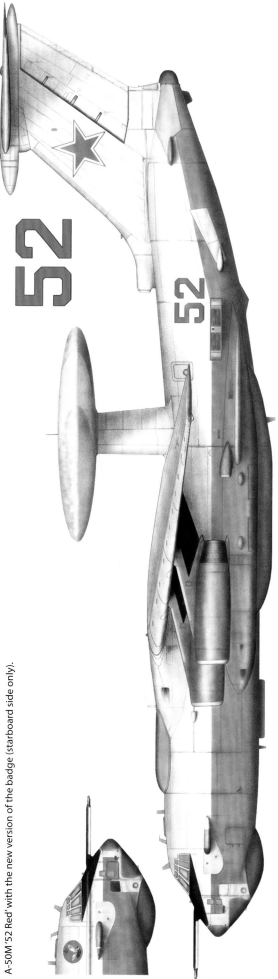

A-50M '52 Red' with the new version of the badge (starboard side only).

A-50U '33 Red'/RF-50602, Zhukovskiy, August 2013.

BBC РОССИИ

RF-50602

ВВС РОССИИ

ВВС РОССИИ

A-50U '37 Red' Sergey Atayants, Ivanovo, March 2014.

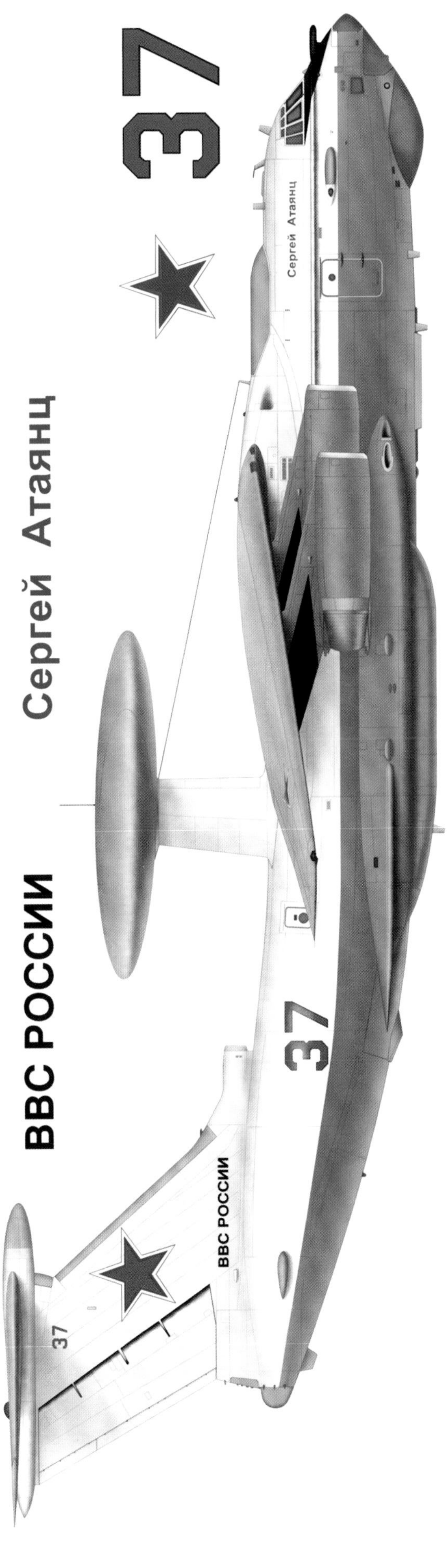

Сергей Атаянц

ВВС РОССИИ

ВВС РОССИИ

Сергей Атаянц

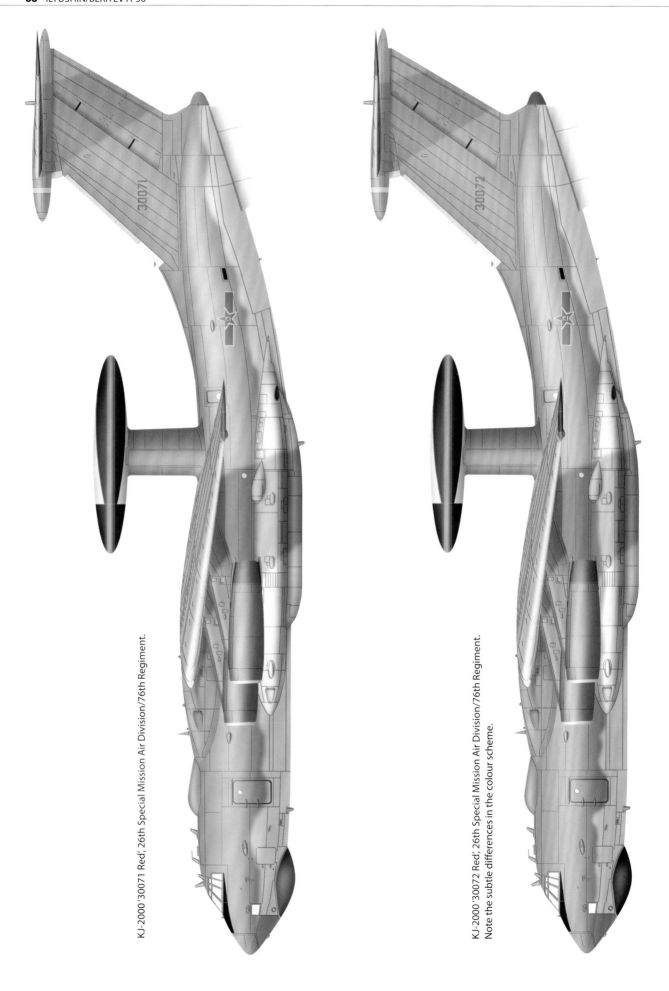

KJ-2000 '30071 Red', 26th Special Mission Air Division/76th Regiment.

KJ-2000 '30072 Red', 26th Special Mission Air Division/76th Regiment. Note the subtle differences in the colour scheme.

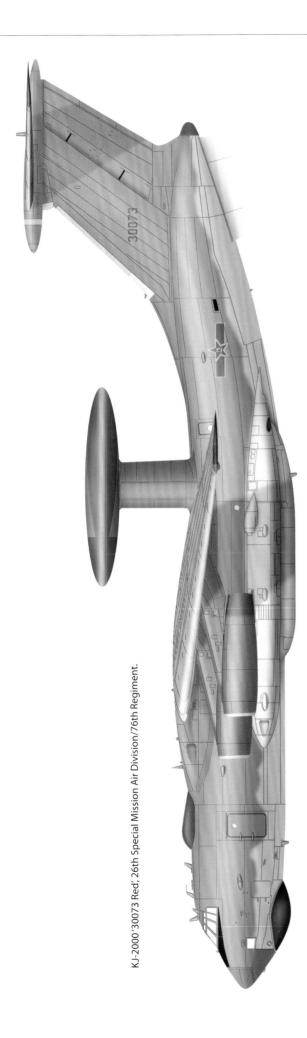

KJ-2000 '30073 Red', 26th Special Mission Air Division/76th Regiment.

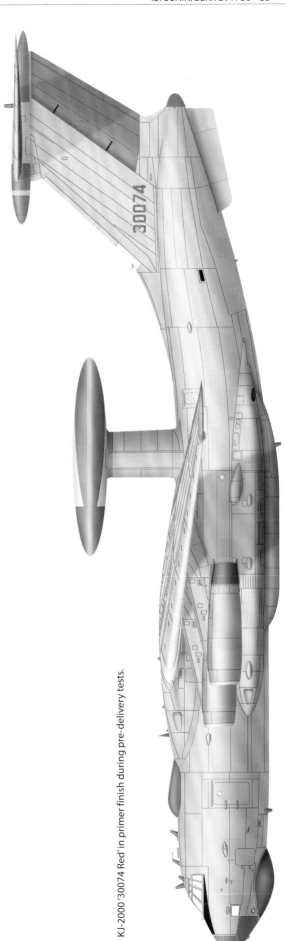

KJ-2000 '30074 Red' in primer finish during pre-delivery tests.

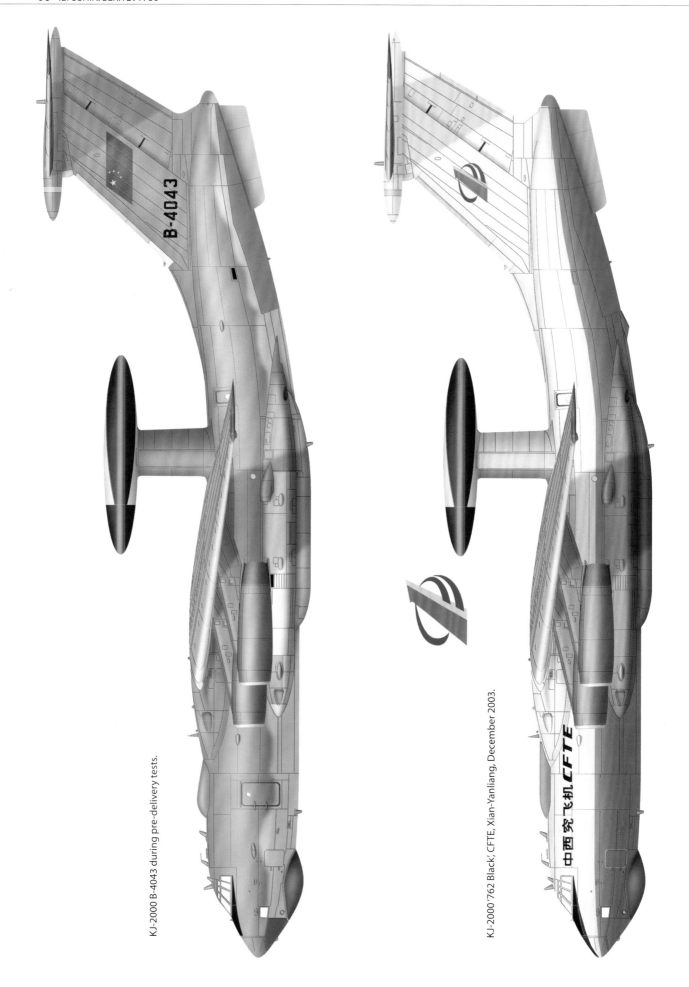

KJ-2000 B-4043 during pre-delivery tests.

KJ-2000 '762 Black', CFTE, Xian-Yanliang, December 2003.

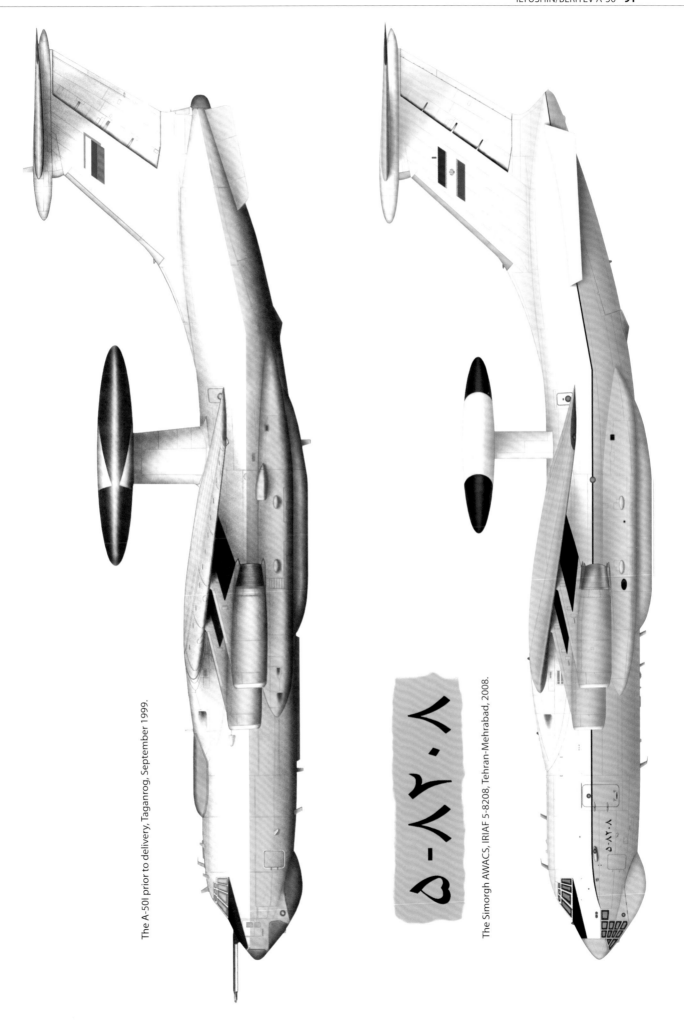

The A-50I prior to delivery, Taganrog, September 1999.

The Simorgh AWACS, IRIAF 5-8208, Tehran-Mehrabad, 2008.

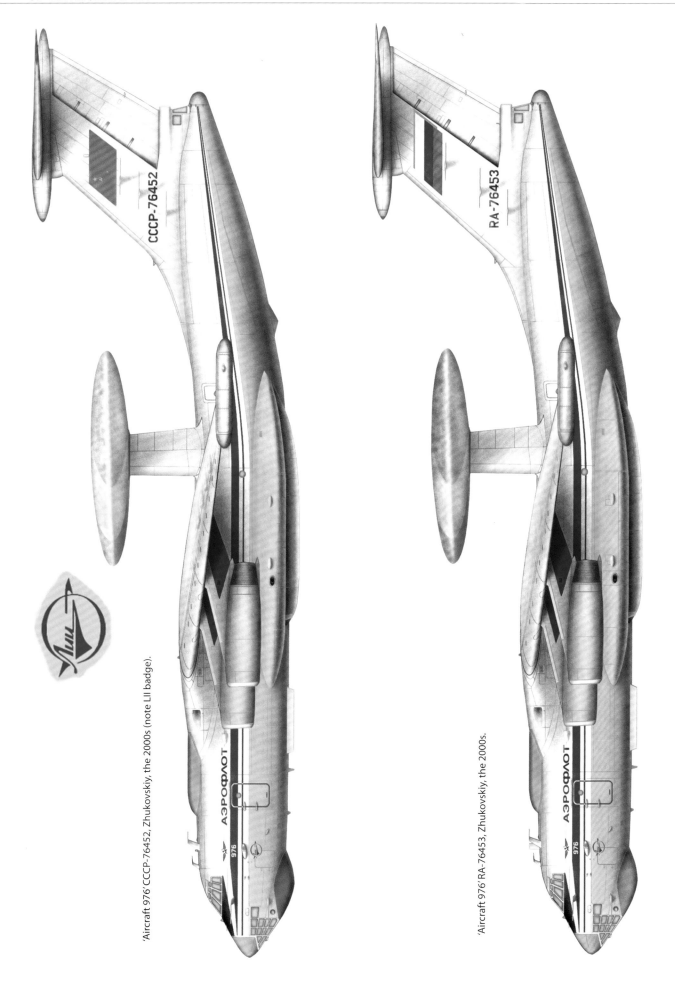

'Aircraft 976' CCCP-76452, Zhukovskiy, the 2000s (note LII badge).

'Aircraft 976' RA-76453, Zhukovskiy, the 2000s.

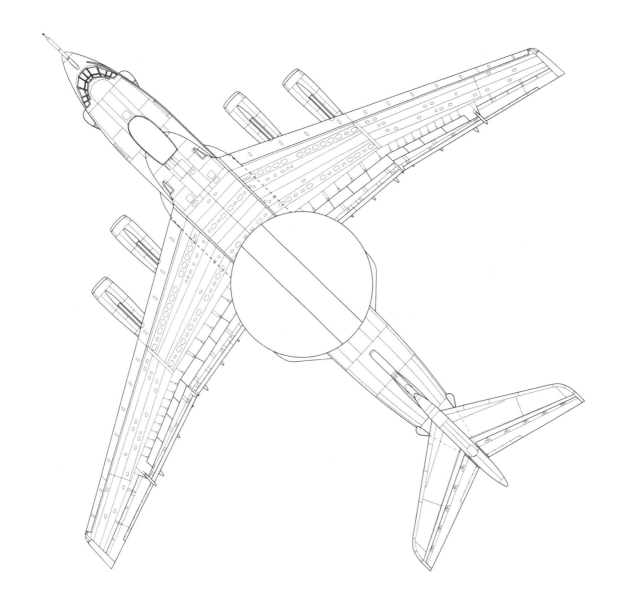

Upper and front views of a
production A-50 *sans suffixe*.

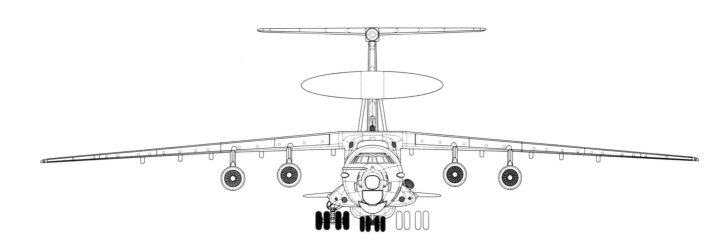

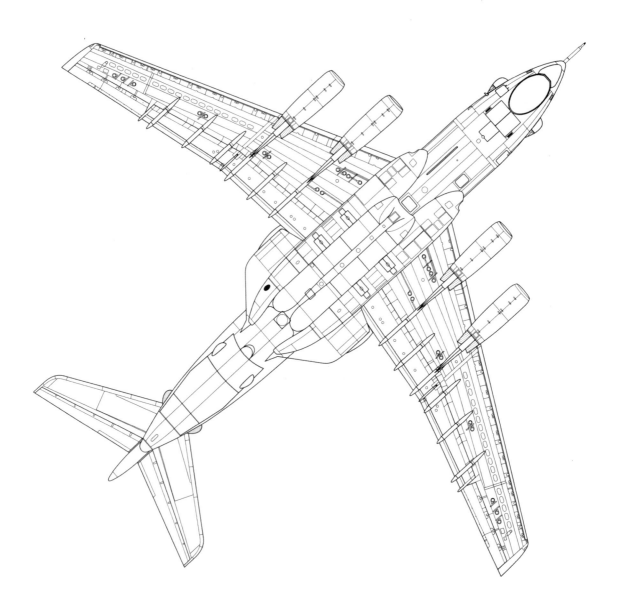

Lower and port side views
of a production A-50M.

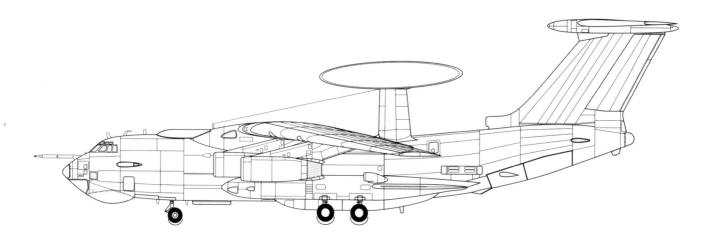

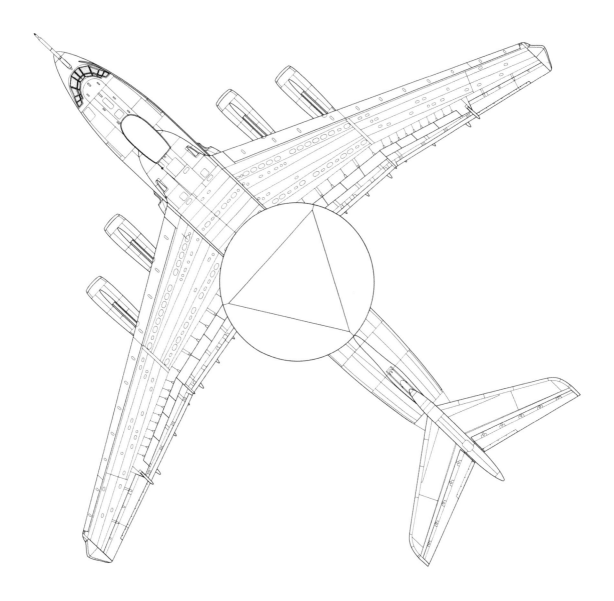

Upper and front views of the A-50I.

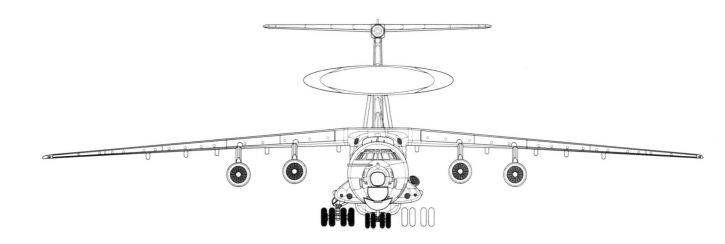

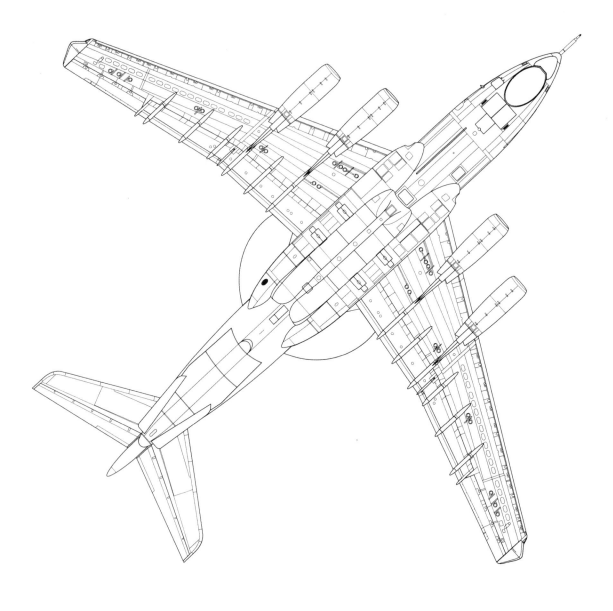

Lower and port side views
of the A-50I.

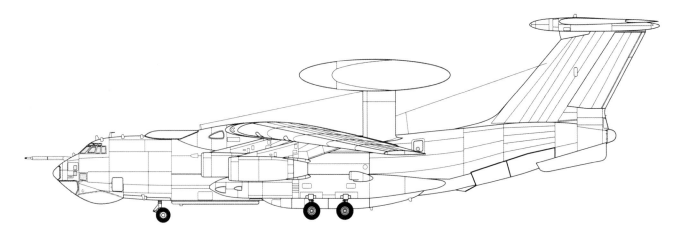